WINE ENTHUSIAST MAGAZINE

Wine & Food

Pairings

COOKBOOK

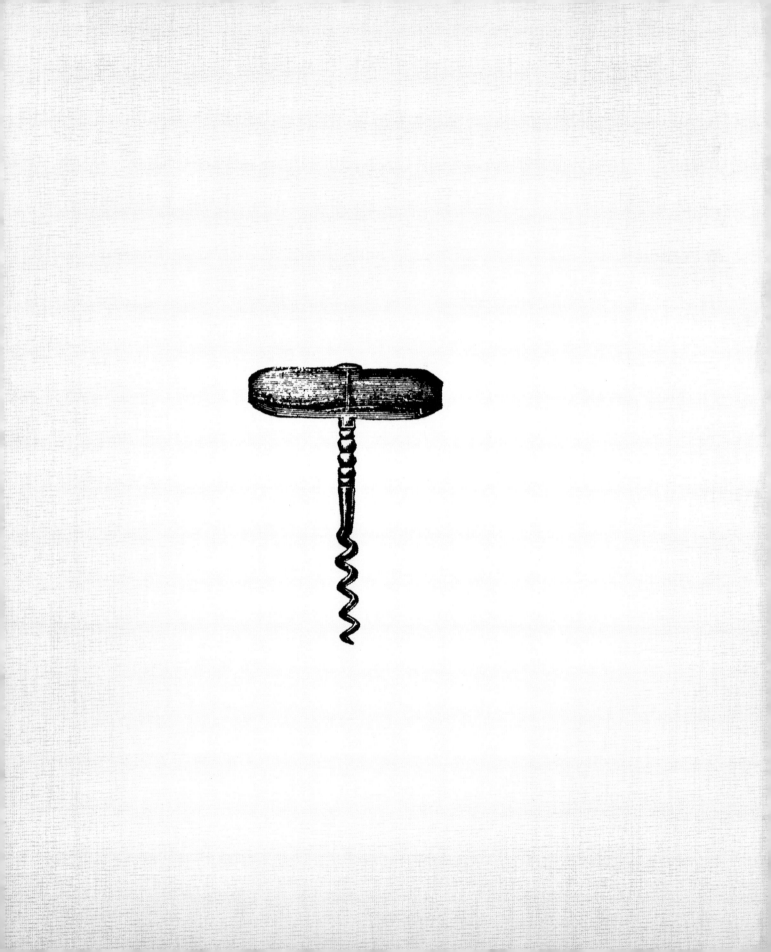

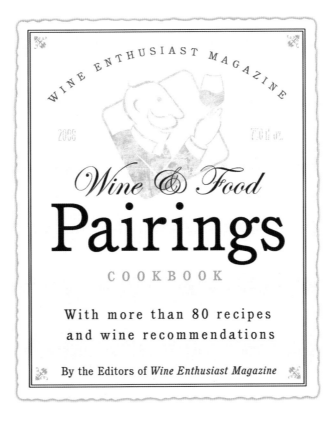

WINE ENTHUSIAST MAGAZINE

Wine & Food

Pairings

COOKBOOK

With more than 80 recipes
and wine recommendations

By the Editors of *Wine Enthusiast Magazine*

FOREWORD BY

Tim Moriarty & Susan Kostrzewa

RUNNING PRESS
PHILADELPHIA • LONDON

Special thanks to Claudine Auguste, Ellen Eden, Evie Righter, and Michael Shachner.

9   8   7   6   5   4   3   2   1
Digit on the right indicates the number of this printing

Library of Congress Control Number: 2008921297
ISBN 978-0-7624-3527-2

Designed by Joshua McDonnell
Edited by Diana C. von Glahn
Typography: Avenir, Cushing, and Edward Script

Photo Credits
Cover, back cover, and inside flap images: Jon Van Gorder

Jon Van Gorder: Pages 18, 22, 25, 26, 34, 37, 46, 48, 50, 59, 62, 73, 79, 90, 102,
105, 113, 114, 121, 122, 125, 129, 137, 139, 147, 149, 158, 165, 169, 170, 173
Dasha Wright Ewing: Page 54
Michael Heintz: Page 71, 88, 179
Monica Larner: Page 75
Courtesy Vintner Grill: Page 77
Bob Capazzo: Page 94

Running Press Book Publishers
2300 Chestnut Street
Philadelphia, PA 19103-4371

Visit us on the web!
www.runningpresscooks.com
www.wineenthusiast.com/magazine

Contents

Wine & Food Pairing Made Easy

The subject of pairing wine with food invites a wide spectrum of attitudes and approaches. At one end of this spectrum is a complete lack of patience for the entire exercise: "I eat what I like, I drink what I like. Just open the bottle and let's dig in." At the other end is the scrupulous search for the ultimate pluperfect pairing, where every nuance of vintage, flavor, body, acidity, tannin, and oak treatment of the wine is scrutinized against the acidity, flavoring, and weight of the base ingredient of the main dish and all its sides—the spicing, saucing, and preparation of everything on the plate, and on the plates of everyone else at the table. At a restaurant, this can involve intense study of the menu and wine list interspersed with keen interrogation of the server and sommelier. Put the two of them at the same dinner table, and chances are, one of them will hit the other with his menu.

At *Wine Enthusiast*, we find merit in both attitudes. For 20 years, *Wine Enthusiast Magazine* has been promoting the philosophy that wine is the perfect accompaniment to food and social ease. We've been steadfast in demystifying wine, taking it off its pedestal, and placing it at the dinner table where it belongs. Still, we understand that wine is an intimidating subject for most people.

The fact is, it *is* intimidating. There are dozens of wine-producing countries, hundreds of grape varieties, thousands of regions, many thousands of producers, strange terms on labels, offputting rituals, and lofty verbiage from professionals. But just because it is an intimidating subject doesn't mean you should be intimidated. To drink the wine you like with the food you've ordered or made is rule one of wine pairing. It overrides all other rules. Therein lies the validity of the "no fuss, drink up" attitude. The truth is, no meal has ever been completely ruined by an "improper" wine and food pairing. So drink what you like.

That's step one in making you a wine expert. But consider this: The wine world is far too rich to drink only what you know you like, and are already familiar with. Exploring that world is part, if not most, of the fun.

The wholehearted search for the perfect pairing is valid, too, as long as the process is, in itself, pleasurable and shared, socially. It's a sensory and intellectual game that can yield spectacular dividends at the table. Make no mistake: The perfect pairing of wine and food is a sublime experience, elevating both to such an extent that the meal will be blissful at the time, and memorable long after.

This book is intended to be a simple, direct, and pleasurable tool to help you get the most from your food and wine choices. Enjoyment and ease are what it's all about. Each chapter's recipes are arranged according to difficulty level, depending on whether you want to present a lavish feast or a quick meal. And the book's chapters are arranged not by food type, but by wine style: Light, Aromatic Whites; Rich, Full-bodied Whites; Rosés and Light Reds; Medium-bodied, Fruit-forward Reds; Big, Powerful Reds; and Sparkling Wines and Dessert Wines. We offer examples of wines in each style and explain why that style of wine will pair with the recipes in that chapter.

"Style" in this context refers to the elements that contribute to the overall feel of the wine in your mouth—viscosity, acidity, tannins, alcohol level, and flavor type and intensity. Even if you're new to wine, all of these terms will be familiar to you except, perhaps, tannins. Tannins, crucial to the aging of fine wines, are chemical compounds found in the skins, seeds, and stems of grapes; some tannins are also incorporated through aging in wood barrels. You will experience tannin, particularly in young, full-bodied red wines, as a sandpapery, drying, astringent feel on your tongue. As a well-made wine ages, the tannins will "melt" and contribute to the more pleasurable, velvety feel in the mouth.

You may be wondering why flavor is taking the back seat to the other components of wine style. After all, when you think of food and drink, flavor is what is foremost on your mind. Two reasons: It is the style—primarily the wine's mouthfeel—that most directly determines its role in regard to food. And mouthfeel is much easier to discern, and much easier to communicate, than flavor. Flavor is subjective. We all are in our own worlds when it comes to flavor. What tastes like citrus to us might have a plummy aspect to you; what we discern as smoke you might taste as mushroom. But style—mouthfeel plus flavor—is something that is more immediate and communicable. Talking about wine style, rather than flavors, will enable you to communicate with your retailer or restaurant sommelier in a common language, so that the bottle reflects your personal preferences and most likely matches what you are planning to serve, if it's a dinner party, or be served if you're at a restaurant. In either setting, knowing your way around this subject, having a vocabulary of wine style, is useful.

To further ease your way into the pairing world, let's cite the much-maligned "white wine with fish, red wine with meat" rule. You will hear it derided because it's very, very old school and there are many, many delicious exceptions to the rule. While this is true on both counts, it remains a useful starting point because it captures the no-fuss, instinctive nature of wine and food pairing we're shooting for.

The basics are these: Pairing is all about matching the main components of the dish and the main components of the wine. By matching, we don't always mean complementing; sometimes a contrasting style is ideal. But in general, think about the main dish's dominant flavor, its character and intensity as well as the comparative level of fats to acids. Then find a wine whose style (acidity, viscosity, tannin, alcohol, and flavor type and intensity) will best showcase that dish. Bullseye. The food and wine will enhance one another, boosting the flavor of each while also, in the best of circumstances, creating a new, pleasurable flavor and sensation.

Thus, white wine with fish: If you've sipped a light Chardonnay or Pinot Grigio, you recall a light texture on the palate and brighter flavors of citrus. Fish: Your sense memories tell you, light (again in color, but also in texture). White meats like chicken and turkey belong in this category. If you do the same mental exercise with a full red wine like Cabernet Sauvignon and a grilled steak, you realize that your sense memories and instincts are telling you that both red wine and red meat–laden plates are fuller, darker, deeper in texture and flavor. And thus, a good pairing.

Of course it's not that simple. Nothing is simple in the wine and culinary worlds. Here's where the exceptions and considerations start flying, and where the fun starts if you're of a mind to explore and ponder.

Just as there is no single way to prepare and serve fish (or meat, or vegetables), there are no useful generalizations possible about the wines of the world: A Chardonnay from Chablis and a Chardonnay from Napa Valley share some core (and quite subtle) flavors and other characteristics, but most of the stylistic elements we discussed will vary widely. This holds true for Pinot Grigio, Sauvignon Blanc, Pinot Noir, Cabernet Sauvignon, Merlot, Syrah, and other wine grapes that are vinified worldwide—the climate, soil, and winery treatments will affect the alcohol, tannins, acidity, intensity, and secondary flavors. And that affects their suitability in pairing with a specific dish.

If fish is simply grilled and served with a light drizzle of olive oil, then a light white wine like most Italian and cool-climate Pinot Grigios is a good match, and so would a lean and steely Chablis. But not all Pinot Grigios or Chardonnays are created equal, as we've seen. A full-bodied, intensely flavored, oaky wine might render the fish tasteless. And what if the fish is not simply grilled and lightly oiled? What if it's smothered in a rich and flavorful cream sauce? In that case, the very light Pinot Grigio might be overwhelmed by the food—the flavor and texture of the dish will mute the wine's flavor or otherwise unfavorably alter it. A fuller white wine or a leaner red like Pinot Noir, might be a better choice. Okay, but what if a squeeze of lemon is needed to bring this fish to life, or perhaps the fish is a component in an acidic ceviche? Then the acidity of the wine becomes a factor; you need either a low-acid wine to contrast with the acidity of the dish or a crisply acidic wine to complement it.

You can see how this can get insane very quickly. So generalizations like "white wine with fish" are useful only to a point. If you leaf through this book, you'll find the answers to many of the questions that naturally arise during this endeavor.

How do I determine the style of the wine from the label?

If you are a complete wine novice, you probably can't, although a pale color, white or red, will hint at some truths, when compared with richer, deeper colors in nearby bottles. As far as the label goes: American wine labels are the easiest, because they will reveal grape variety, region, and alcohol content. European wine labels are most difficult, because . . . well, just take a stroll through the France or Germany aisle of your wine store; you get the idea. In short, it's difficult to glean what you want from a wine label unless you already have a familiarity with the major wine regions of the world and at least a grasp of the major wine grape varieties. At the intersection of the two is the information you want. This book will give you the tools to ask useful questions of your retailer or sommelier. The day of the snobby sommelier is over; most people in the wine world are happy to help. If they give you attitude, it's their problem, not yours.

Each chapter contains a description of the style covered therein and the wine classification chart in the back of the book categorizes varieties by style. A section in the

"Big, Powerful Red Wines" chapter, for example, will explain what that term means, how alcohol content, tannins, oak treatment, and, of course, grape variety contribute to that character. It will give examples of wine grapes and regions that are most closely associated with the style, and some general cuisines and specific dishes that pair well with it.

What if I'm looking for a wine to pair with a pasta dish, or a stew, or one of those nouveau cuisine dishes with many assertively flavored components in the dish?

You need to consider the overall impression of the dish on the palate; the lamb, chicken, beef, fish, or vegetables will likely take on the character of the seasoning or at least take a back seat to the overall texture. To put it another way: What is the dominant element? If it's a stew, is it tomato-based, and therefore acidic? (Try a fresh, aromatic white like Sauvignon Blanc or a light, easygoing red like Lambrusco.) Is it more earthbound, featuring mushrooms, garlic, and onions, as in many sautéed dishes? (Try a medium-bodied, fruit-forward red like Pinot Noir.) If it's a pasta, is it a creamy sauce or a leaner, oil-based sauce? Some refined dishes and ethnic cuisines, like Thai, call for citrus flavorings. Much vegetarian cuisine is herbal in nature. Each of these will point you to a certain style of wine, and you will find it easily here through perusing recipes or the material pertaining to that style of wine. (One useful shortcut, though: Many such dishes are regional and you should definitely think in terms of the regional wines. An Italian pasta? Italian wine.)

What if the dish is extremely spicy and hot?

The richness of the dish will partially determine this, but in general, you want a low alcohol, high acid wine with some sweetness (fresh, aromatic whites). The acidity blends with the heat, while the sweetness will help mitigate, rather than accent, the heat. (A high alcohol wine will accent the dish's heat, and the flavor of the wine will be muted.) Riesling and Gewürztraminer are the classic choices for Chinese food, but for barbecue, consider a big, powerful red, such as Zinfandel or Shiraz, red wines with some faint spice notes. You won't find the word "beer" in this book, but, let's be honest, that works too.

How about very rich, fatty dishes?

Fried foods, in particular, are a case when you want a crisp, light wine (fresh, aromatic white) to cut through the oil. In effect it cleanses your palate and allows you to taste the fish or chicken. Sometimes you want to contrast, not complement, the dish and the wine. If the dish is creamy and rich, it might render a rich, creamy wine like a warm-climate Chardonnay flabby; you might want an acidic wine to cut the richness and allow both flavors to shine. A lamb or beef dish swimming in a rich, nuanced sauce might call for a big, powerful red wine to showcase those flavors.

Grilled meats?

Grilling imparts a smoky flavor, obviously, but also an earthiness to meats. Choose A rich, full-bodied white wine for grilled chicken or fish, or a big, powerful red, like Zinfandel, for grilled red meat.

Vegetable dishes?

Two factors are important here: the richness of the dish (are the vegetables presented in a cream sauce or does dairy otherwise makes an appearance?) and cooked vs. raw. If dairy enriches the dish, then a richer wine is called for—but this is a relative term here; fresh, aromatic whites with a touch of sweetness will generally pair well. Stay in the comfort zone of Rieslings and Pinot Grigios for whites or light, easygoing reds like Beaujolais. Are your root vegetables cooked (they'll be on the earthy side, so try a full-bodied white like many Chardonnays) or raw? Mushrooms are of course earthy in flavor, so a Pinot Noir might match.

Vegetables, like asparagus and artichokes, comprise some of the classic "difficult pairing" dishes. We deal with those in our Never Say Never recipes and pairings. A Never Say Never pairing is one that defies common sense or assumption, partnering typically difficult or bold foods like the mildly metallic asparagus with wines that soften or enhance, or two foods that might not typically be paired together, i.e. red wine and fish.

Are you sure this is fun?

It is, if you want it to be. And it's important, in this sense: If you are having friends for dinner, you want them to enjoy your cooking and appreciate the wines you serve without necessarily seeing the effort and thought behind them. What if you unwittingly serve a wine that makes your Veal Oscar taste like a heel cushion, or if your Sole Meuniere makes the wine you present taste like skid-row jug juice? We exaggerate, of course. As we said before, no meal has been completely ruined by an improper pairing, but why not enhance your chances of brilliance and triumph? Time spent with this book, and consideration of the outstanding recipes, will improve your odds.

We want to share our enjoyment with the wine and food dynamic without boring you. And we hope you will do the same, without taxing your guests or tablemates or making yourself frantic. Wine has shed its image as elitist and intimidating. It's all about enjoyment, from this time forward.

Cheers,

Tim Moriarty
Managing Editor

Susan Kostrzewa
Senior Editor

Chapter 1

Light, Aromatic
White Wines

The recipes we've paired with light, aromatic white wines are truly pleasing. They are tempting, too. If you were contemplating which of them to order at your favorite bistro or neighborhood eatery, you would be hard-pressed to choose just one. The burger with Thai saté sauce? The tostadas with chicken and citrus slaw? The Vietnamese steak salad? Or, maybe, the mussels Provençal?

Much of the allure of these dishes is their variety; many are international. You can choose from among French, Italian, Spanish, and Asian cuisines. Even more than the types of cuisines, though, it is the uncomplicated flavors and methods that make these dishes so pleasurable. Like the wines that accompany them, the food is simply enjoyable—fun to make, good to eat. The recipes are easy and versatile. You can serve them for lunch, a summer supper on the patio, or an informal get-together with friends around a big kitchen table.

Should you be on the lookout for more of a "main" course, we have a few of those here, too: paella of chicken and seasonal mushrooms; avocado, tomato, and spinach crêpes with bacon and pesto; linguine with shellfish and the lightest of tomato sauces; and, last but not least, a party dish of pork loin with a heavenly cider-Madeira sauce that will serve up to twenty people.

For those who want to pair a glass of wonderful wine with just a small bite, we have just the recipe: crispy fried artichokes—made as only the Italians know how—are a taste of the sublime with a glass of Verdicchio dei Castelli di Jesi or Soave Classico.

Think of this chapter, too, as just the first tempting taste of a delicious feast of food and wine pairings to come.

Mussels Provençal

SERVES 4 AS A MAIN COURSE, OR 6 OR MORE AS A SIDE

The beauty of cooking with mussels these days is that farm-raised mussels are widely available and so easy to prepare. Already washed and trimmed, they make repeated cleanings a thing of the past.

SAUCE

2 teaspoons olive oil

4 tablespoons butter

6 garlic cloves, finely chopped

12 plum tomatoes, coarsely chopped

1 pint grape tomatoes

1 tablespoon chopped fresh parsley

1 tablespoon chopped fresh oregano or ¼ teaspoon dried

½ tablespoon chopped fresh basil

MUSSELS

4 pounds mussels

1 teaspoon vegetable oil

2 tablespoons butter

1 shallot, finely chopped

1 garlic clove, finely chopped

2 cups dry unoaked white wine, such as Sauvignon Blanc

Crusty bread, for serving

Ease of Preparation: Easy to Moderate

To make the sauce: Heat the oil and butter in a large skillet over medium-high heat. Add the garlic and cook, stirring, for 30 seconds to 1 minute, or until soft and translucent. Add all the tomatoes and cook for 5 to 10 minutes, until they soften and break down. Break up the tomatoes with a spoon if necessary. Stir occasionally to prevent sticking. Cover and set aside.

To steam the mussels: Sort through the mussels, discarding any that are open or that do not close when you tap them. Wash and remove the stringy beard from any that need it.

Heat the oil and butter in a large pot set over medium-high heat until the butter is melted. Add the shallot and garlic and cook, stirring, for 30 seconds to 1 minute, or until translucent and soft. Add the wine and bring to a simmer.

Add the mussels, cover the pot tightly, and cook for about 5 minutes, or until all the mussels have opened. Discard any that do not open. Using a slotted spoon, transfer the mussels to a bowl and set aside. Return the steaming liquid to the heat and cook until syrupy and reduced in volume.

Return the tomato sauce to the heat; stir in the mussel cooking liquid and the parsley, oregano, and basil. Add the mussels to the sauce and stir gently. Serve hot, with crusty bread.

> **PAIRING** Crisp and clean but fruity wines pair well with the freshness of this dish, such as Sauvignon Blanc from Chile, South Africa or New Zealand; recommended producers include Terrunyo or Montes (Chile), Neil Ellis (S. Africa), and Cloudy Bay (NZ).

Totally Nuts Chicken Saté Burgers

SERVES 4

Traditional Thai seasonings of curry and peanuts work flawlessly with chicken burgers.

SATÉ SAUCE

½ cup peanut or vegetable oil

2 garlic cloves, minced

1 teaspoon curry powder

½ cup unsalted dry-roasted peanuts, finely chopped

BURGERS

1 pound ground chicken (breast or blend of breast and dark meat)

¼ cup unseasoned bread crumbs

2 tablespoons finely chopped yellow onion

1 large egg, lightly beaten

Salt and freshly ground black pepper

Vegetable oil for the grill

4 sesame seed rolls, halved

Ease of Preparation: Easy

To make the saté sauce: Heat the oil in a medium saucepan over medium heat; add the garlic, and simmer for 1 minute, then add the curry powder and the peanuts. Simmer for about 5 minutes longer, until the sauce has a peanut butter–like consistency. Pour the sauce into a heatproof bowl and set aside.

To make the burgers: Start a charcoal grill and build a medium-hot fire; preheat a gas grill to medium-high; or preheat your broiler and move the oven rack to the second-highest level.

In a bowl, combine the ground chicken, bread crumbs, onion, and egg, then season with salt and pepper. Form 4 equal patties, taking care not to compress the meat too much. Brush the grill lightly with oil and grill the burgers for 5 minutes or more on each side, or until the juices run clear, the burgers are firm to the touch, and the internal temperature is 175°F or above on a thermometer.

To serve, place each burger on a sesame roll bottom and top with a generous spoonful of saté sauce and the top half of the roll. Serve immediately, passing the remaining sauce separately at the table.

NOTE: For food safety, be sure to cook the burgers until they are well-done and reach the recommended internal temperature.

> **PAIRING** The curry and peanuts in this dish call for a wine that has both structure and acidity, such as an unoaked Chardonnay from Australia or New Zealand; recommended producers include Grant Burge, The Witness Tree, and Tohu (NZ).

Spaghetti with Cockles and Parsley

SERVES 4 TO 6

This variation on the classic *spaghetti alle vongole* is adapted from *The Flavors of Southern Italy* by Erica De Mane. In her Italian-American home, De Mane grew up eating this dish on Christmas Eve.

3 pounds cockles or Manila clams, scrubbed clean

¾ cup dry white wine

2 tablespoons kosher or sea salt, plus more as needed

1 pound spaghetti or linguine

⅓ cup extra virgin olive oil, plus additional for drizzling

3 garlic cloves, thinly sliced

Grated zest and juice of 1 lemon

Freshly ground black pepper

½ cup coarsely chopped flat-leaf parsley

PAIRING The clams and lively citrus in this spaghetti play off the rich, lemony character of a Fiano di Avellino or Greco di Tufo; recommended producers include Feudi di San Gregorio, Mastroberardino, Terredora, and Villa Matilde.

Ease of Preparation: Moderate

Cover the cockles with cold water and soak for 20 minutes. Lift out the cockles; if any sand remains, soak them again until the water is devoid of sand.

Place the cockles in a large saucepan and add the wine. Turn the heat to medium, cover the pan, and cook until the cockles open, about 5 to 10 minutes. Using a slotted spoon, transfer the cockles to a bowl and cover them to keep warm. Reserve the cooking liquid.

Meanwhile, bring 6 quarts of cold water and the salt to a boil in a large pot. Add the spaghetti, stir, and cook until al dente, about 10 minutes.

Meanwhile, heat the olive oil in a large skillet over medium-low heat. Add the garlic and sauté until it is light golden. Pour half of the reserved cockle cooking liquid into the skillet. Add the lemon zest and juice, and let the sauce bubble for a minute or two.

Add the cockles with the remaining cooking liquid to the skillet. (If the skillet is not large enough, pour the sauce over the cockles.) Taste and add additional salt if needed; season with pepper.

Drain the spaghetti and return it to the pot. Add a generous drizzle of olive oil and the parsley; toss well.

To serve, spread the pasta on a platter or divide it among shallow soup bowls. Top it with cockles and sauce. Serve immediately.

Wild Mushroom Hunter's Soup

SERVES 6 TO 8

This recipe is adapted from *Cooking One-on-One: Lessons from a Master Teacher* by John Ash. The original recipe was actually tossed together on a canoe trip using foraged ingredients, but unless you are feeling jaunty and are a wild mushroom expert, this version works equally well with store-bought exotic mushrooms. Any flavorful cultivated mushroom, such as shiitake, oyster, hen of the woods, portobello, and the like could be used.

4 tablespoons olive oil

2½ cups thinly sliced onions

2 tablespoons thinly sliced garlic

1½ pounds fresh trumpet royale and alba clamshell cluster mushrooms, wiped clean and thickly sliced

1½ cups fresh tomatoes, diced, or canned diced tomatoes in juice

6 cups chicken or mushroom stock, or canned low-sodium chicken broth

⅓ cup amontillado Sherry

2 tablespoons finely grated lemon zest

Salt and freshly ground black pepper

Freshly grated Parmesan or Asiago cheese, for serving

Fresh parsley, chives, basil and/or chervil, chopped, for garnish

Ease of Preparation: Easy to Moderate

Heat 2 tablespoons of the olive oil in a large, deep saucepan over medium-low heat. Add the onions and garlic and cook for 10 to 15 minutes, stirring, until they are light golden.

While the onion mixture is cooking, heat the remaining 2 tablespoons of olive oil in a separate pan over high heat; add the mushrooms and sauté until they are cooked through and lightly browned. Add the sautéed mushrooms, tomatoes, and stock to the onion mixture. Bring to a boil, then reduce the heat and simmer for 3 to 4 minutes. Stir in the Sherry and lemon zest and season to taste with salt and pepper.

Serve the soup in warm bowls or mugs, garnished with a sprinkling of grated cheese and chopped fresh herbs.

PAIRING The earthiness of the mushrooms combined with zesty ingredients like lemon, garlic, and onion make the fruity yet clean flavors of a California Sauvignon Blanc a sure bet; recommended producers include Selene, Gainey, and Rochioli.

Chilled Cucumber Water with Minted Crab Salad

SERVES 4

Chef Michael Allemeier of Mission Hill Family Estate in British Columbia's Okanagan Valley created this soup. It is best when made with fresh, peak-of-the-season cucumbers from the farmers' market or the garden. Get started the night before you plan to serve the soup to allow enough time for the cucumbers to render their liquid.

4 large cucumbers

1 leek

1 head fennel, trimmed and chopped

2 tablespoons chopped fresh dill

1 tablespoon sea salt

4 ounces cooked fresh Dungeness crabmeat

1 tablespoon mayonnaise

1 tablespoon fresh mint chiffonade (see Note)

1 teaspoon finely grated fresh ginger

SPECIAL EQUIPMENT: cheesecloth

Ease of Preparation: Moderate

The day before you plan to serve this soup, wash the cucumbers well and halve them lengthwise. (Don't peel them.) Using a spoon, scrape out all the seeds. Dice the cucumber and transfer it to the bowl of a food processor.

Cut the green leaves off the leek and, holding the root end, slice it lengthwise almost to the root. Wash it well to remove all sand. Cut off the root, remove any remaining green leaves, and dice the white part. Add the diced leek, fennel, dill, and salt to the food processor and purée until smooth.

Place a large piece of cheesecloth in a bowl so that the corners hang over the sides. Pour the cucumber mixture onto the cheesecloth. Collect all the ends of the cloth and tie them together to form a bag. Tie the ends to a shelf in the refrigerator and place a bowl under the bag so the liquids can drain through the cheesecloth. Refrigerate overnight.

The next day, gently squeeze the cheesecloth bag to release any remaining liquid; discard the bag and its contents. Strain the liquid through a fine-mesh sieve into another bowl. Taste and season with salt if necessary. Chill until ready to use.

Combine the crab, mayonnaise, mint, and ginger in a bowl; mix well, taste and season with salt, if necessary. Using your hands, form 4 small balls of crab salad, 1 tablespoon each. For a more refined version, use 2 spoons to shape the crab salad into *quenelles*: take one spoon in each hand, then scoop about 1 tablespoon crab salad onto one spoon, cover it with the other spoon, and shape it into an oval.

Pour the cucumber water into 4 chilled soup bowls. Gently place a *quenelle* into the center of each bowl and serve immediately.

NOTE: For a chiffonade, make a stack of the mint leaves, then roll up the stack; using a sharp knife, cut the roll crosswise into thin strips, or ribbons.

Vietnamese-Style Steak Salad

SERVES 4

While this stir-fried beef and rice noodle salad is fantastic at home, it makes great picnic fare. The beef-noodle combination marinates in a resealable plastic bag as you make your way to the picnic, while the greens and vegetables, packed separately in a covered plastic container, stay cool and crisp, awaiting a mealtime toss with the soy-lime dressing that's been stored in a jar.

4 ounces rice noodles (vermicelli)

⅓ cup soy sauce

3 tablespoons fresh lime juice

1 tablespoon sugar

1 teaspoon finely chopped garlic

½ teaspoon red pepper flakes

1 pound sirloin steak, well trimmed

2 tablespoons vegetable oil

1 small head Boston or butter lettuce, shredded (about 5 cups)

1 cucumber, halved lengthwise, seeded, thinly sliced

½ cup grated peeled carrot

½ cup fresh mint leaves

Ease of Preparation: Moderate

In a small saucepan, cook the noodles in boiling water until soft, about 3 minutes. Drain and rinse. Transfer the noodles to a medium bowl and set aside to cool.

In a small jar, combine the soy sauce, lime juice, sugar, garlic, and pepper flakes; cover the jar and shake until the dressing is well combined.

Slice the steak against the grain into thin strips.

Heat the vegetable oil in a wok or large skillet over medium-high heat. Add the steak in batches and stir-fry until just cooked through. Transfer the beef to the bowl with the noodles; add half the dressing and toss until well coated. Set aside to cool and allow the flavors to come together.

Combine the lettuce, cucumber, carrot, and mint in a bowl.

Just before serving, toss the greens with the remaining dressing and divide among 4 plates. Top each with the beef-noodle salad.

PAIRING An Alsatian or domestic Gewürztraminer, with its spicy, floral character, tempers but doesn't drown the kick of salt and spice in this dish. Recommended Alsatian producers include Zind-Humbrecht, Marc Kreydenweiss, Trimbach, and Domaines Schlumberger; recommended domestic producers include Sineann and Navarro.

Chicken and Citrus Slaw Tostadas

SERVES 6

New Yorker Paula Disbrowe left city life behind and moved to a Texas ranch in 2002. Her cookbook, *Cowgirl Cuisine*, from which these *tostadas* are taken, chronicles her journey from city girl to cowgirl, and is full of down-home recipes with cosmopolitan touches. The Spanish word *tostada* literally means "toasted," while the dish refers to a fried tortilla loaded with a variety of toppings.

2 to 3 cups vegetable oil, for frying

6 (6-inch) corn tortillas

3 ounces firm tofu, diced

¼ cup fresh lime juice

2 tablespoons red wine vinegar

1 tablespoon honey

1 tablespoon Dijon mustard

1 canned chipotle chile in adobo (see Note)

¼ cup vegetable oil

2 teaspoons finely grated orange zest

1 teaspoon finely grated lime zest

Kosher salt and freshly ground black pepper

½ small green cabbage, finely shredded (3 cups)

¼ small red cabbage, finely shredded (1½ cups)

1 small red onion, thinly sliced

1 large carrot, finely grated

3 tablespoons finely chopped fresh cilantro

3½ cups shredded cooked chicken (from 1 medium roastchicken, skin removed)

Lime wedges, for garnish

Additional chopped chipotle chiles in adobo, for garnish

Ease of Preparation: Moderate

In a small skillet, heat ½ inch of oil over medium heat until hot but not smoking. Place a tortilla in the hot oil and fry until golden and crisp, turning once, about 2 minutes. Transfer the *tostada* (fried tortilla) to paper towels to drain. Repeat with the remaining tortillas.

Combine the tofu, lime juice, vinegar, honey, mustard, and chipotle chile in a food processor or blender and process until smooth. While the processor or blender is running, add the ¼ cup vegetable oil in a thin stream and process until creamy. Transfer to a bowl. Stir in the orange and lime zest and season with salt and pepper to taste.

Toss the cabbages, onion, carrot, and cilantro in a large bowl and season with salt and pepper. Add all but 3 tablespoons of the dressing and toss.

To serve, set the *tostadas* on plates and mound the slaw on top. Add the chicken to the empty slaw bowl, toss with the reserved 3 tablespoons dressing, and mound atop the slaw. Garnish each *tostada* with lime wedges and additional chipotle peppers in adobo. Serve.

NOTE: Chipotle chiles in adobo can be hot. If you are sensitive to spicy food, begin by adding half a chipotle, taste, and either stop there, or add the remaining chile. Canned chipotle chiles in adobo can be found in the Latin foods section of many supermarkets.

PAIRING An off-dry Vouvray (Chenin Blanc) has enough curviness to balance the tartness in these tostadas, but its acidity matches the lime and vinegar notes well; recommended producers include Château Moncontour and Domaine Huët.

Chicken and Seasonal Mushroom Paella

Paella de Polloy Setas

SERVES 4 TO 6

This recipe is from José Andrés, founding chef and co-owner of three Jaleo restaurants in the Washington, D.C. area, as well as four other Spanish and Latin-influenced eateries. Andrés says his classically inspired paella pays homage to bygone days **when chick**ens were something special, and the dishes that featured them were the centerpiece of a feast. *Sofrito* is the sauce that launched a thousand dishes. It's the essence, the foundation of Spanish cooking. It's a meeting of the Old World of olive oil and the New World of tomato that makes the perfect basis for any starring ingredient—chicken, fish, or shellfish. You'll use this recipe again and again in tapas cooking. Master it, commit it to memory, and open the door to Spain.

SOFRITO

10 ripe plum tomatoes

1 ½ cups Spanish extra-virgin olive oil

4 small Spanish onions, peeled and chopped fine, about 4 cups

1 teaspoon sugar

1 teaspoon pimentón (Spanish sweet paprika)

1 bay leaf

Salt

PAELLA

2 tablespoons extra virgin olive oil

2 chicken legs, cut into small pieces

8 ounces fresh wild mushrooms, such as chanterelles

3 ounces green beans, cleaned and cut into 1-inch pieces

½ garlic clove, finely chopped

2 tablespoons chopped *jamón Serrano* (Spanish dry-cured ham)

¼ cup dry white wine

¼ cup *sofrito*

4 cups chicken stock or canned low-sodium chicken broth, plus additional if needed

1 pinch saffron

1 bay leaf

1 tablespoon salt

1½ cups Spanish Bomba rice or Arborio rice

Ease of Preparation: Moderate

To make the *sofrito*: Cut the tomatoes in half. Place a grater over a large mixing bowl. Rub the open face of the tomato into the grater until the flesh is gone. Discard the skin. Strain the mixture.

Heat the oil in a medium saucepan over a low to medium flame. Add the onions and the sugar. Cook for 45 minutes, stirring occasionally with a wooden spoon, until the onion becomes soft and tender with a light brown color. You want the onions to caramelize. If the onions get too dark, add ½ tablespoon water to keep cooking the onion evenly without burning.

Add the reserved tomato purée, the pimentón, and the bay leaf. Cook for another 20 minutes at a medium heat. You'll know your sofrito is ready when the tomato has broken down and deepened in color, and the oil has separated from the sauce. Add salt to taste.

To make the paella: Heat the olive oil in a paella pan or another large, shallow skillet over high heat. Add the chicken and sauté until it is brown on all sides, about 4 minutes. Transfer the chicken to a plate and set aside.

Add the mushrooms to the pan and sauté until they are golden, about 3 minutes. Add the green beans and garlic, and cook for 3 minutes. Return the chicken to the pan along with the ham. Pour in the wine and cook until it reduces by half, about 1 minute. Add the *sofrito* and cook for 3 minutes. Add the stock and bring to a boil. Crush the saffron and add it to the pan along with the bay leaf and salt. (The mixture should be just a little salty; when you add the rice, the seasoning will balance itself out.)

Add the rice, taking care to spread it evenly around the pan. Cook over high heat, stirring frequently with a wooden spoon, for 5 minutes. The rice should float in the liquid in the pan. If it is not floating, add an extra ½ cup stock or water. Reduce the heat to low and maintain a slow boil for 10 minutes, until the liquid is absorbed. Do not put your finger or a spoon into the paella again or the rice will cook unevenly.

Remove the paella from the heat and let it sit for 3 minutes. At this stage, the stock should be absorbed by the rice and there should be a nice shine to the top of the paella. Serve immediately.

NOTE: Chef Andrés points out that you can make the sofrito several days in advance and store it in an airtight container in your refrigerator. The key to this sauce is the onion, not the tomato. Make sure the onion is cooked well enough that it's soft and sweet—sweet enough to smell— before you add the tomato. Then use your judgment with the seasoning, including the sugar. This sauce should become something you always want to keep on hand, mastered and committed to memory. You'll use it time and again to great effect. You can also add extra vegetables to this paella, such as eggplant, zucchini, or cauliflower, to the paella. For the best flavor, be sure to sauté the vegetables after sautéing the chicken. You can also add chicken livers for extra flavor, or substitute rabbit for the chicken.

PAIRING Highly aromatic with ample acid, wines like Godello or a fuller-bodied Albariño complement the salty, rich, and savory flavors of this paella. Recommended Godello producers include Guitían and Viña Godeval; recommended Albariño producers include Pazo Señorans and Do Ferreiro.

Linguine with Shrimp, Scallops, and Clams in Light Tomato Sauce

Linguini all' Istriana

SERVES 6

This dish comes from Lidia Bastianich, the celebrated host of television's "Lidia's Italy" and "Lidia's Family Table", and author of their companion cookbooks. It is deliciously briny when the shellfish is at its freshest. The tomatoes give it complexity, and the hot pepper flakes add a spicy kick.

15 littleneck clams

½ pound sea scallops

6 tablespoons olive oil

6 large garlic cloves, crushed

2 cups crushed peeled tomatoes

1 teaspoon red pepper flakes

3 tablespoons sea salt

1½ pounds linguine

1 pound medium shrimp, heads removed, peeled, and deveined

3 to 4 tablespoons chopped fresh flat-leaf parsley

SPECIAL EQUIPMENT: shucking knife

Ease of Preparation: Moderate to Difficult

Freeze the clams for 20 minutes to relax the muscle that clamps their shells together.

Meanwhile, cut off and discard the hard little white nubbin attached to the side of each scallop, then cut the scallops in half horizontally. Set aside.

To shuck the clams, work over a bowl to catch the juices. If you are right-handed, hold a clam in the palm of your left hand (opposite if you're left-handed), with the hinge end facing you. Hold the shucking knife in other hand and place its point between the shells at the opening end. With the clam secure in your left hand, carefully force the knife between the shells and cut around under the top shell to release the clams. Rotate the blade between the shells to force them open. Run the blade under the body of the clam to release and remove it. Pour any juices into the bowl. Repeat with the remaining clams.

Chop the clams and place them in a separate bowl; set aside.

Heat 2 tablespoons of the olive oil in a sauté pan over medium heat. Add the garlic and cook until it browns very

lightly. Add the tomatoes and pepper flakes and simmer for 20 minutes.

While the sauce is simmering, bring 6 quarts of water to a boil in a stockpot. You want to time it so that the water is at a full boil by the time the shellfish is ready. Add the salt, then stir in the linguini and cook until it is al dente, 7 to 9 minutes.

While the pasta cooks, heat 2 tablespoons of the olive oil in a sauté pan over medium-high heat. Stir in the shrimp and scallops and sauté for 30 seconds, until any liquid has evaporated. Stir in the clams and clam juice, being careful not to include any sand that might be at the bottom of the bowl. Raise the heat to high and shake the pan until the liquid comes to a boil. Add more pepper flakes, if desired.

Pour in the tomato sauce and return the mixture to a boil, shaking the pan. Check the seasoning again, then add the remaining 2 tablespoons of olive oil and stir in the parsley.

Drain the cooked pasta and toss immediately with the hot sauce. Serve immediately.

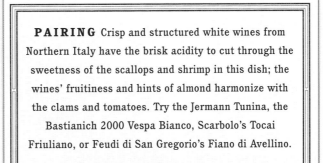

PAIRING Crisp and structured white wines from Northern Italy have the brisk acidity to cut through the sweetness of the scallops and shrimp in this dish; the wines' fruitiness and hints of almond harmonize with the clams and tomatoes. Try the Jermann Tunina, the Bastianich 2000 Vespa Bianco, Scarbolo's Tocai Friuliano, or Feudi di San Gregorio's Fiano di Avellino.

Pork Loin with Cider-Madeira Sauce

SERVES 20, WITH 4 CUPS SAUCE

This recipe, which is adapted from a recipe found on cooks.com, makes enough sauce for a large gathering. However, you can serve fewer guests simply by using a smaller roast. Allow about one-half to three-quarter pounds of meat for each person.

GLAZE

2 garlic cloves, finely chopped

½ teaspoon salt

3 tablespoons molasses

1 teaspoon freshly ground black pepper

PORK AND SAUCE

4 tablespoons vegetable oil

1 boneless pork loin (8 to 10 pounds)

1 (750ml) bottle hard cider

1 (750ml) bottle Madeira

½ pound shallots, finely chopped

1 whole allspice

1 cup beef broth

¼ cup cornstarch dissolved in ⅓ cup cold water

3 tablespoons unsalted butter, cut into pieces

2 tablespoons Dijon mustard

Salt and freshly ground black pepper

Ease of Preparation: Moderate

To make the glaze: Mash or purée the garlic and salt into a paste, using either the flat side of a knive blade, a mortar and pestle, or a food processor. Transfer the paste to a small bowl, mix in the molasses and pepper, and set aside. (The glaze can be made in advance and stored, covered, at room temperature for up to 8 hours.)

Preheat the oven to 325°F.

To roast the pork loin: In a large, heavy roasting pan that can be used on the stovetop as well, heat the oil over high heat until it ripples. Add the pork loin and brown each side. Remove the pork loin from the pan, place a roasting rack in the pan, and place the pork loin on the rack, fatty side up. Roast for 20 minutes per pound, or until a meat thermometer inserted into the thickest part reads 165°F. Brush with glaze twice during roasting. Remove the pork from the oven and let it rest for a few minutes.

To make the sauce: While the pork is roasting, combine the cider, Madeira, shallots, and allspice in a heavy saucepan and simmer over medium-low heat until the liquid is reduced by half.

When the pork loin is done, transfer it to a serving platter. Deglaze the roasting pan by adding the broth and stirring to scrape up any browned pork bits. Pour the broth into a 2-cup measure and skim off the fat. Add the skimmed broth to the cider-Madeira mixture and bring to a boil. Whisk in the cornstarch mixture and simmer for 2 minutes. Whisk in the butter until it melts. Remove the pan from the heat and whisk in the mustard. Strain the sauce into a clean saucepan, season with salt and pepper, and transfer to a gravy boat for serving.

> **PAIRING** The gamut of Alsatian white wines, with their apple crispness, mirror the cider in the sauce and slight sweetness of the pork; recommended producers include Zind-Humbrecht, Domaine Weinbach, Paul Blanck, and Josmeyer.

Avocado, Tomato, and Spinach Crêpes with Bacon and Pesto

MAKES 12 TO 16 CRÊPES; SERVES 4 AS A MAIN DISH OR 8 AS AN APPETIZER

These rich crêpes are excellent when paired with a crisp green salad. Prepare the crêpes and pesto ahead of time to make the assembly easier.

CRÊPES

1 cup all-purpose flour

2 large eggs

1¼ cups milk

¼ teaspoon salt

2 tablespoons melted butter

2 tablespoons butter

PESTO

2 cups packed fresh basil leaves

¼ cup grated Romano or Parmesan cheese

¼ cup pine nuts or walnuts

2 garlic cloves

½ cup olive oil

Salt and freshly ground black pepper

FILLING

6 strips bacon

1 large tomato, seeded and diced

4 cups baby spinach

¼ cup finely chopped red onion

4 ounces smoked Gouda or provolone cheese, shredded

1 large or 2 small avocados, diced

Ease of Preparation: Difficult

To make the crêpes: combine the flour, eggs, milk, salt, and melted butter in a blender and blend until smooth. Cover and refrigerate for at least 30 minutes, or up to overnight, to allow air bubbles to escape.

Heat a 6- or 7-inch nonstick crêpe pan or skillet over medium heat. Melt 1 teaspoon butter in the pan.

Gently stir the batter, then ladle or pour 2 to 3 tablespoons of batter into the center of the pan, tilting the pan to cover it completely. Cook the crêpe until the edges begin to turn brown, about 1 minute. Turn the crêpe over and cook another 15 seconds. Invert the crêpe onto a plate. Repeat the cooking process, adding more butter to the pan as needed and adjusting the heat so the crêpes don't burn. Stack the cooked crêpes on a plate. To make the crêpes ahead of time, store them, already cooked, in the refrigerator between layers of wax paper for up to 2 days or in the freezer (tightly sealed in plastic wrap and foil) for up to 2 months. Reheat before using.

To make the pesto: Combine the basil, cheese, pine nuts, and garlic in a food processor or blender, and chop thoroughly, stopping every now and then to push the basil down. With the motor running, add the olive oil in a steady stream and blend until thoroughly combined. Season with salt and pepper.

To make the filling: Cook the bacon until crisp in a skillet set over medium heat. Using a slotted spoon, transfer the bacon to paper towels to drain. Crumble the bacon and set aside.

Drain the bacon grease from the skillet (don't wipe out the skillet) and add the tomato, spinach, and red onion. Cook, stirring, over medium heat until the spinach is wilted and

the tomatoes are warm, about 4 minutes. Remove the skillet from the heat and stir in the bacon, cheese, and avocado.

To assemble: Preheat the oven to 400°F. Butter a 13 x 9-inch ovenproof dish.

Arrange the crêpes on your work surface and spread about 2 teaspoons of pesto on each crêpe. Spoon equal amounts of filling in the center of the crêpes and roll them up. Place the crêpes in the prepared dish and bake until warmed through, about 5 minutes.

PAIRING A New World-style white like New Zealand Sauvignon Blanc has enough dimension to balance the richness of this dish without weighing it down; recommended producers include Kim Crawford, Villa Maria, and Brancott.

Crispy Fried Artichokes

SERVES 4

This recipe is adapted from Anna Dente Ferracci's recipe for whole fried artichokes served at her celebrated restaurant, Osteria di San Cesario, outside of Rome. Ferracci and her mother, known as Sora Anna ("sister Ana") and Sora Maria, are queens of the Italian fried artichoke.

10 tender, small artichokes with stalks

Juice of 1 lemon

4 cups extra virgin olive oil

All-purpose flour, for coating

Salt

Ease of Preparation: Easy to Moderate

To prepare the artichokes: With the artichoke on its side, cut off the top half and discard. You should see tender yellow leaves and the pink spiky choke at the center. Snap off the tough, dark green outer leaves until you reach the tender ones. With a knife, cut off the woody skin on the outside of the stalk, leaving about two inches from the base. Halve the artichokes lengthwise, then quarter them and remove any thistly parts. Cut them into eighths or thin wedges and place in a large bowl of water with freshly squeezed lemon juice. (Artichokes oxidize when cut, causing them to turn brown; putting them in lemon water will prevent this.)

To fry the artichokes: Heat the oil in a fryer or large, heavy pot over low heat. The oil is ready when a drop of water crackles and fizzles to evaporation: never let the oil get so hot that it starts to smoke.

Coat a ceramic plate with flour. Gently press the moist artichoke wedges directly into the flour so they are covered evenly. Place the artichokes in the oil in batches to avoid overcrowding, and fry until crisp and golden. Using a slotted spoon, transfer the artichokes to paper towels to drain briefly. Arrange the artichokes on a serving platter, season lightly with salt, and serve immediately.

NEVER SAY NEVER **PAIRING**

The high acidity of a Verdicchio dei Castelli di Jesi or Soave Classico mirrors the leanness of lemon and artichoke, while the nuttiness rounds out the dish and gives it dimension. Recommended Verdicchio producers include Fazi Battaglia, Sartarelli, and Umani Ronchi; for Soave, try Pieropan, Gini, and Tommasi.

Pesto alla Genovese

SERVES 4; MAKES ABOUT 1 CUP PESTO, ENOUGH FOR 1 POUND PASTA

Pesto originated in the Italian province of Liguria. Its capitol, Genoa, is honored in the name of this dish, which is made all over the city. Chef Antonio Amato, originally from Naples but happily transplanted to Genoa, makes some of the best pesto in town. Most Genovese cooks prefer to use pesto with *trenette*, or little twisted braids of pasta, but Antonio opts for *picage* (from the local dialect's word for "napkin") instead. This is a flat, lasagna-type pasta, cut into rough, large squares that fold onto themselves and trap the pesto within. Here, we use lasagna noodles cut into pieces. He also uses less garlic than is customary because he considers its taste too strong; garlic lovers can add more if desired. Many Ligurian chefs insist that a mortar and pestle is the best tool for making pesto, but if you prefer, a food processor works very well. They also favor Ligurian olive oil, which is more delicate than oils from elsewhere in Italy. If you can't find it, your favorite extra virgin oil will work just fine.

Ease of Preparation: Easy to Moderate

Place the basil, garlic, and pine nuts in a mortar and lightly grind them into a paste with the pestle; or if you prefer, place them in a food processor and process until fairly smooth, stopping the machine to scrape down the sides as necessary. Let the mixture sit for a few minutes to allow the flavors to marry, then add the cheese and mix or process until evenly combined. Continue to mix or process as you add the oil in a thin stream.

Bring a large pot of water to a boil. Add a generous pinch of salt and then the pasta. Boil the pasta until it is al dente, about 10 minutes. Drain the pasta, then arrange the strips on a work surface and cut into 4-inch squares.

In a bowl, toss the pasta with about ½ cup pesto. Continue to add the pesto in ½ cup increments, tossing after each addition, until the pasta is coarsely coated. Serve immediately.

NOTE: Cubed boiled potatoes and cooked string beans are sometimes added to this dish.

---

2 cups tightly packed fresh young basil leaves

1 garlic clove

¾ cup pine nuts

½ cup freshly grated Parmesan cheese, preferably Parmiggiano-Reggiano

½ cup olive oil, preferably a light-colored Ligurian oil

Salt to taste

1 pound lasagna noodles

NEVER SAY NEVER PAIRING

With its crisp apple and orange flavors and dry but rich mouthfeel, the Sardinian white wine Vermentino plays well with the brisk basil and garlic in this dish; recommended producers include Guado al Tasso, Capichera, and Santadi.

About Light, Aromatic Whites

Most would agree that a light, aromatic white wine conveys the essence of freshness, a lack of thickness on the palate, and the complete nonexistence of oak-driven aromas and flavors. Light, aromatic wines tend to come from cooler wine-growing climates that generally sit close to the ocean. These wines are made from grapes harvested earlier in the fall (September in the northern hemisphere, March in the southern hemisphere), which are fermented and then aged entirely or almost entirely in neutral vessels, which impart no additional flavors to the wine. Stainless steel tanks are the most common.

Arguably the most quintessential light, aromatic whites are the Sauvignon Blancs from New Zealand, Chile, and France's Loire Valley. These wines feature lively acidity, aromas and flavors of green and tropical fruits, and even some minerality. What they don't offer is unctuous aromas, palpable body weight, and strong notes of vanilla, butter, and toast. And the list of light, aromatic whites goes on and on to include wines from Austria, the west and east coasts of Italy, Galicia in Spain, Alsace in France, the Cape Winelands of South Africa, and even the countryside of southern England.

As the name implies, aromas are a key component of wines made from Sauvignon Blanc, Riesling, Pinot Grigio, Gewürztraminer, Pinot Blanc, Fiano di Avellino, Falanghina, Garganega, Verdicchio, Vermentino, Godello, Albariño, Verdejo, Muscadet and even Chardonnay (if it is grown in a cool area and not aged in oak). Such wines have an undeniable cleanness that can conjure memories of fresh fruits, a grassy meadow, a mountain stream, or even the inside of an oyster shell. These wines are blessed with the acidity necessary to refresh and cleanse the palate, and because they are almost always unoaked, which relieves a winery from having to invest in expensive barrels, they tend to be much lower in price than their richer, fuller-bodied brethren.

With light, aromatic whites, you should always seek the newest vintage possible, assuming that the vintage is of good quality. And these wines are not meant to be aged, which is why a good many of them are now being sealed with screwcaps as opposed to corks: freshness and early access are what they are all about.

As for food pairings, the best matches for light, aromatic whites tend to be chilled soups, shellfish, salads, grilled fish, chicken, and Asian/Indian foods. Spice is not the enemy of these wines, thus foods like Thai saté and the hot chili peppers that go into Chinese, Caribbean, and Mexican cooking will not overpower the wines.

Chapter 2

Rich, Full-Bodied
White Wines

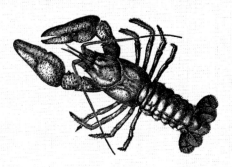

If the recipes that best accompany the fresh, aromatic white wines of Chapter 1 are easy to like and generally informal, the foods that pair best with rich, full-bodied white wines are just the opposite. The bar has been raised. That bottle of exceptional white wine you've been reserving for a special occasion can find its match in recipes of equal complexity presented here.

Stylish starters and elegant main courses prevail. Not surprisingly, shellfish stars in this chapter, and these recipes are is the best of the catch. Lobster is showcased in two remarkably smart, distinctive combinations, while Dungeness crab and oysters are also featured. If fish is your pleasure, there is whole snapper grilled with fennel and served with ratatouille, and a one-of-a-kind warm salad of tuna confit. If the ingredients sound luxe, they are, and their preparation is often multi-step and sophisticated. Subtlety is at work in this chapter, and intrigue abounds. Just as the wines in this chapter have haunting, complex qualities, so does the food.

That doesn't mean you need to be a star-worthy chef to attempt the following recipes. Three chilled soups require only a minimum amount of culinary expertise, but reward with a maximum amount of flavor. Better still, each has make-ahead components. And, if you are of the school that holds to the notion that a superb meal starts with a silken, hot cream soup, we have two recipes you're sure to enjoy.

Our advice: begin by browsing through this chapter. Even if you don't cook the recipes right away, it will make fantastic reading. But if you're feeling ambitious, pick out the starter and entrée that will complement that big bottle of white in your collection, the one that's just begging to be opened. Then turn to Chapter 7: You'll need a dessert to end your knockout meal.

Chilled Corn Soup with Crab and Scallion

SERVES 4 AS A STARTER

This soup was a featured Recipe of the Month in the July 2006 issue of *Wine Enthusiast Magazine*. It is one of a trio of summertime soups—the other are also in this chapter—that Chef Jeff Raider serves in Martini glasses at Valley Restaurant at the Garrison in Garrison, New York. Recipes for the other two soups in the trio follow this one.

1 teaspoon extra virgin olive oil

½ small Vidalia onion, coarsely chopped

1 garlic clove, coarsely chopped

2¼ cups chicken stock or canned low-sodium chicken broth

1¼ cups fresh corn kernels (from about 2 medium ears)

Salt and freshly ground black pepper

4 pieces jumbo lump crabmeat

1 scallion, thinly sliced

Ease of Preparation: Easy

Heat the olive oil in a medium nonreactive pot over medium heat. Add the onion and garlic, and cook until soft, 3 to 5 minutes. Do not allow them to brown.

Add the stock and bring the mixture to a boil, then reduce the heat and simmer for 3 minutes. Add the corn and return to a boil, then reduce the heat and simmer for 4 to 6 minutes, or until the corn is tender.

Working in batches if necessary, transfer the soup to a blender and purée until smooth. Alternately, blend the soup with an immersion blender. Season with salt and pepper, then pour the soup into a nonreactive container and chill until cold.

To serve, ladle the soup into stemmed glasses or small soup cups and garnish each serving with crab and scallion.

> **PAIRING** Australian Chardonnay, with its creamy texture and balanced flavors of oak and stone fruit, holds its own against the creamy crab and corn elements of this cool starter; recommended producers include Vasse Felix, Henschke, and Grosset.

Tomato Gazpacho with Avocado and Lobster

SERVES 4 AS A STARTER

This version of gazpacho—the classic Spanish chilled summer soup—by Chef Jeff Raider at Valley Restaurant at the Garrison in Garrison, New York, gets added color and richness from garnishes of lobster and avocado. Get started one day before you plan to serve the gazpacho to give the soup time to chill and allow the flavors to blend.

2 ripe tomatoes, seeded and chopped

1 cucumber, peeled, seeded, and chopped

1 red jalapeño pepper, seeded and chopped

1 red bell pepper, seeded and chopped

1 yellow bell pepper, seeded and chopped

1 red onion, chopped

1 garlic clove, chopped

1 teaspoon fresh lime juice

1 tablespoon Sherry vinegar

3 tablespoons extra virgin olive oil

½ cup V-8 juice

1 tablespoon chopped fresh mint

1 tablespoon chopped fresh cilantro

Salt and freshly ground black pepper

1 ripe avocado, diced

1 tablespoon cooked lobster meat, diced

Ease of Preparation: Easy

Combine ½ cup cold water, the tomatoes, cucumber, jalapeño, bell peppers, onion, garlic, lime juice, vinegar, oil, V-8, mint, and cilantro in a food processor and pulse until well blended. Season to taste with salt and pepper. Transfer the mixture to a plastic container, cover, and refrigerate overnight.

Pour the tomato mixture into a blender and process on high speed until smooth.

To serve, ladle the gazpacho into stemmed glasses or small cups and garnish each serving with avocado and lobster.

PAIRING The fresh citrus and pineapple flavors of a white Bordeaux complement the tangy tone of this mouth-puckering soup; recommended producers include Château La Louvière, Château Carbonnieux, and Château Smith-Haut-Lafitte.

Maine Lobster Salad

SERVES 4

This recipe is from David Daniels, executive chef of Topper's Restaurant at The Wauwinet in Nantucket, MA. With lobster as as the main attraction, this dish is in keeping with Chef Daniels' commitment to showcasing regional ingredients.

4 (1-pound) lobsters

1 cup diced celery

½ cup mayonnaise

1 tablespoon chopped flat-leaf parsley

1 tablespoon chopped shallot

1 tablespoon olive oil

1 teaspoon white truffle oil

1 teaspoon fresh lemon juice

½ teaspoon sea salt

¼ teaspoon white pepper

6 cups mixed baby greens

2 slices brioche, toasted and cut into triangles

Ease of Preparation: Moderate

Cook the lobsters in a large pot of boiling salted water for about 8 minutes, until the shells are bright red. Plunge the lobsters into a pot of ice water to stop the cooking and quickly cool them. Remove all the meat from the lobster, then cut the meat into bite-size pieces.

In a large bowl, combine the celery, mayonnaise, parsley, shallot, olive oil, truffle oil, lemon juice, and salt and pepper. Add the lobster meat and combine gently. Spoon the lobster salad into a small ring mold or ramekin and pack it down lightly.

To serve, spread the greens on a serving platter. Invert the mold onto the greens. Garnish with the brioche triangles. Alternatively, the lobster salad can be spooned atop greens on individual plates.

NOTE: Small, one-pound lobsters are also known as chicken lobsters.

PAIRING Fruity and full-bodied, a California Chardonnay from Napa or Sonoma County will mirror the richness of ingredients like this soup's white truffle oil, lobster, and mayonnaise; recommended Napa producers include Newton and El Molino; recommended Sonoma producers include Gallo of Sonoma, Williams-Selyem, and Dutton-Goldfield.

Garlic and Portobello Soup with Goat Cheese and White Truffle Oil

SERVES 4

Chef Cal Stamenov of Marinus Restaurant at the Bernardus Lodge in Carmel Valley, California, created this elegant and creamy soup of mushroom, garlic, and a hint of apple-smoked bacon. It somehow just begs for a spot next to a crackling fire when the weather outside is crisp.

5 shallots, sliced

1 head garlic, cloves separated, peeled, and sliced

1 medium leek, cleaned and sliced in ½-inch pieces

2 slices apple-smoked bacon, cut into ½-inch pieces

5 portobello mushrooms (each about 6 inches in diameter) with stems, diced

1½ cups Pinot Noir

2 cups chicken stock or canned low-sodium chicken broth

2 cups heavy cream

Salt and freshly ground black pepper

Garlic croutons, for garnish

4 tablespoons crumbled goat cheese, for garnish

White truffle oil, for garnish

Garlic flowers, for garnish, optional

Ease of Preparation: Easy to Moderate

Cook the shallots, garlic, leek, and bacon in a large, covered, heavy saucepan over medium-low heat, shaking the pan occasionally, until the shallots and garlic are translucent, 10 to 15 minutes. Add the mushrooms, cover the pan, and cook until most of the moisture from the mushrooms evaporates, 5 to 10 minutes. Add the wine, increase the heat to medium-high, and cook until the liquid reduces by three-quarters, 5 to 7 minutes. Add the stock and reduce the heat to low, bringing the soup to a slow simmer. Add the cream and bring just to a boil. Working in batches if necessary, transfer the soup to a food processor and purée. Alternately, use an immersion blender to purée the soup. Pour the soup into a heatproof bowl, and season with salt and pepper. Pass the soup through a fine-mesh sieve into a clean saucepan and keep warm over low heat.

To serve, ladle the soup into soup bowls and garnish with garlic croutons, 1 tablespoon of the goat cheese, 5 drops of truffle oil, and garlic flowers.

> **PAIRING** The brown-butter creaminess of a Monterey County Chardonnay pairs well with the apple-smoked bacon and mushrooms in this decadent dish; recommended producers include Bernardus, Morgan, and Mer Soleil.

Summer Squash Soup with Basil and Parmesan

SERVES 4

This vegetarian recipe is adapted from a recipe in *Keep It Seasonal: Soups, Salads and Sandwiches* by Annie Wayte. It relies on zucchini, fresh herbs, and grated Parmesan for its appealing color and flavor.

2 tablespoons extra virgin olive oil, plus more for drizzling

3 pounds zucchini, trimmed and cut into ½-inch dice

3 shallots, finely diced

1 garlic clove, minced

3 cups vegetable stock

1 cup heavy cream

1 bunch fresh basil leaves, coarsely chopped

1 bunch fresh mint leaves, coarsely chopped

8 tablespoons freshly grated Parmesan cheese

Sea salt

Freshly ground black pepper

Ease of Preparation: Easy to Moderate

In a large saucepan, heat the olive oil over medium heat. Add the zucchini and sauté for about 12 minutes, until it is lightly colored. Add the shallots and garlic and sauté for 5 more minutes. Add the stock and bring to a boil. Reduce the heat and simmer for 5 minutes. Remove the pan from the heat.

Working in batches if necessary, transfer about two-thirds of the soup to a blender or food processor and purée. Return the purée to the remaining soup in the pan and set it over low heat. Add the cream and reheat the soup, stirring continually to prevent the soup from burning. Stir in the basil, mint, and cheese until well combined. Taste and season with salt and pepper, if necessary.

Ladle the soup into 4 bowls and finish with a generous drizzle of extra virgin olive oil. Serve immediately.

PAIRING With its dry, vibrant qualities and steely core, a Puligny-Montrachet offers the kind of layered but delicate character that can match the assertive flavors here but not overpower them; recommended producers include Etienne Sauzet, Louis Jadot, and Domaine Leflaive.

Chilean Crab Casserole

Pastel de Jaibas

SERVES 8

This recipe melds *pastel de jaibas* recipes from Rodríguez and Jorge "Coco" Pacheco, chef and owner, respectively, of Santiago's renowned seafood restaurant Aquí Esta Coco. The *aji chileno*, a fresh hot pepper seasoning called for in the recipe, must be made a day in advance. When working with hot chiles, it is a good idea to wear protective gloves.

AJI CHILENO

10 jalapeño peppers

1 cup white wine vinegar

1 cup vegetable or olive oil

1 garlic clove

CASSEROLE

4 cups fresh white bread crumbs without crusts, processed to crumbs in a food processor

2 cups milk

2 tablespoons olive oil

2 tablespoons butter

1 cup chopped onion

2 to 3 garlic cloves, minced

1 teaspoon paprika

1 teaspoon dried oregano

½ teaspoon ground cumin

Salt and freshly ground black pepper

½ cup dry white wine

½ cup fish or shellfish stock

1½ pounds crabmeat, picked over

1 cup heavy cream

⅔ cup grated Parmesan cheese

Ease of Preparation: Moderate

To make the *aji chileno*: Cut the jalapeño peppers in half lengthwise, discarding all or almost all of the seeds. Put them in a small, nonreactive bowl, add the vinegar, and cover; marinate overnight to soften the skins.

Drain off the marinade and combine the peppers, oil, and garlic in a food processor; pulse to purée. Transfer the purée to a covered container and reserve.

To make the casserole: Combine the bread crumbs and milk in a large bowl; set aside.

Heat the olive oil and the butter in a large skillet over medium-high heat. Add the onion, garlic, paprika, oregano, cumin, and salt and pepper, and sauté until the onion is translucent. Add the wine, and deglaze the pan for 2 to 3 minutes, scraping up the cooked bits from the bottom of the pan. Stir in the stock, then add the crabmeat, bread-milk mixture, and cream. Cook for 5 minutes, stirring the entire time. Stir in 2 teaspoons of *aji chileno*, or more to taste. Check the overall seasonings and adjust to taste. The mixture should be moist and creamy, but not runny. If it is too runny, let the mixture simmer for another 5 minutes, until it thickens.

Preheat the oven to 400°F.

Spoon the crab mixture into 8 individual gratin dishes. Sprinkle with Parmesan cheese and bake until golden brown, about 5 to 8 minutes. Serve immediately.

NOTE: *Pastel de Jaibas* is traditionally baked in a large clay pot, called a *pomaire* in Chile, after the artisan town that specializes in producing them. Intrepid chefs can also bake the mixture in the empty crab shells.

PAIRING With its lively, medium-bodied character of citrus and apple, Chilean Chardonnay will match the zesty and creamy components of this dish; recommended wines include Casa Lapostolle's Cuvée Alexandre, Montes Alpha, and Amelia from Concha y Toro.

Grilled Whole Red Snapper
with Grilled Fennel and Ratatouille

SERVES 6

This recipe, which is adapted from one by Chef Rick Moonen, makes a stunning presentation. The accompaniments of fresh grilled fennel and ratatouille are perfect complements for a summer meal.

SNAPPER

1 whole (4- to 6-pound) red snapper, scaled, gills removed, gutted, rinsed, and patted dry

Freshly ground white pepper

1 teaspoon sliced garlic

1 tablespoon coarsely chopped fresh flat-leaf parsley

1 to 2 teaspoons extra virgin olive oil, plus additional for grilling

½ lemon, sliced into ¼-inch-thick half-moons

1 teaspoon dried oregano

¼ teaspoon red pepper flakes

FENNEL

1 fennel bulb

2 tablespoons olive oil

2 tablespoons fresh lemon juice

Salt and freshly ground black pepper

RATATOUILLE

4 tablespoons olive oil

1 onion, diced

1 red bell pepper, seeded and diced

1 yellow bell pepper, seeded and diced

1 small eggplant, peeled, seeded, and diced

1 zucchini, peeled, seeded, and diced

1 yellow squash, peeled, seeded, and diced

Salt and freshly ground black pepper

2 tablespoons finely chopped shallot

2 tablespoons finely chopped garlic

1 tablespoon fresh thyme leaves

1 cup diced seeded plum tomatoes

Ease of Preparation: Difficult

To marinate the snapper: Using a sharp knife, make three shallow incisions on each side of the snapper. Place it in a stainless steel roasting pan or rimmed baking sheet and season with white pepper. Place the garlic, parsley, olive oil, lemon slices, oregano, a pinch of white pepper, and the red pepper flakes in a bowl and mash them together with your hands, combining all the juices. Lightly massage the marinade into the snapper, being careful of the dorsal fin, which can be very sharp. Cover and refrigerate for 1 to 2 hours.

To make the ratatouille: Heat the olive oil in a large sauté pan over medium-high heat until the oil ripples. Add the onion, stir to coat with oil, and cook, stirring frequently, for 1 minute. Add the bell peppers and cook, stirring, for 2 minutes. Add the eggplant, and cook, stirring, for 2 minutes. Add the zucchini and squash, season with salt and pepper, and cook, stirring, for 2 more minutes, or until all the vegetables are soft. Add the shallot, garlic, and thyme, stir to combine well, and cook for another 2 minutes. Add the tomatoes and cook just until heated through. Keep warm until ready to serve.

To make the fennel: Trim off the tough outer pieces. Slice the bulb lengthwise into "stalks" ½-inch thick (so that each piece consists of bulb and stalk). Transfer the slices to a bowl and drizzle with the olive oil and lemon juice. Season with salt and pepper and set aside.

To cook the snapper: Rub the grill rack with oil, and preheat a gas grill to high; or if you are using a charcoal grill, leave one section of the grill with no coals under it. When the coals turn white, the grill is ready. Wipe out the cavity of the snapper with a paper towel (excess oil can spill and cause flare-ups) and place it on the grill. Grill for 2 minutes, until the fish is lightly charred. Turn the fish over by grasping it between a flat, long-handled spatula underneath and the side of a long-handled fork on top, being careful not pierce the fish with the fork. Grill for 2 more minutes, until charred. When both sides are charred, reduce the temperature of the gas grill or move the snapper to the side of the grill without coals directly below. Cover the grill and let the snapper cook for 4 to 5 minutes, or until the flesh inside the cavity is opaque, not translucent.

Meanwhile, grill the fennel for about 2½ minutes, turn, and grill the other side for 2½ minutes, or until the fennel is lightly charred. Remove from the grill.

When the snapper is done, place it on a serving platter and surround it with fennel and ratatouille. Serve immediately.

PAIRING A round, Rhône-style white blend with a balance of grassy flavors and honeyed fruit will enhance and temper the acid and spice of this dish; recommended wines include Torbreck's Marsanne-Viognier-Roussanne blend from Australia, Châteauneuf-du-Pape Blanc from Château Le Nerthe, or Treana's Rhône-inspired white from the Central Coast of California.

Sweet Pea Soup with Warm Lardons

SERVES 4 AS A STARTER

Chef Jeff Raider at Valley Restaurant at the Garrison in Garrison, New York, combines fresh peas with pea leaves and fresh mint for this singularly colored summer soup. Pea leaves are available in farmers markets, specialty shops and some supermarkets, but can be hard to find out of season. If you can't locate them, double the amount of fresh peas instead.

1 teaspoon extra virgin olive oil

1 scallion, coarsely chopped

1 garlic clove, coarsely chopped

2¼ cups chicken stock, canned low-sodium chicken broth, or water

1¼ cups fresh peas

1¼ cups tightly packed fresh pea leaves

14 fresh mint leaves (no stems)

Salt and freshly ground black pepper

¼ pound slab bacon, chopped into small pieces

Ease of Preparation: Easy

Heat the olive oil in a medium nonreactive pot over medium heat. Add the scallion and garlic and cook until soft. Do not allow them to brown.

Add the stock and bring to a boil. Add the peas and simmer until they are tender, 5 to 10 minutes. Transfer the mixture to a blender and process on high speed until smooth. Add the pea and mint leaves and process again until smooth. Season with salt and pepper. Transfer the soup to a nonreactive container, cover, and refrigerate until chilled.

Just before serving, cook the bacon until crisp in a small skillet. Use a slotted spoon to transfer it to drain on paper towels.

To serve, ladle the soup into stemmed glasses or small cups and garnish each serving with bacon.

PAIRING An oaked Sauvignon Blanc from France's Loire Valley offers both creamy complexity and freshness, matching those elements in this soup; recommended producers include Didier Dagueneau in Pouilly-Fumé, and Lucien Crochet and Pascal Jolivet in Sancerre.

Wrapped Oyster Fritters with Apple-Mint Chutney and Passion Fruit Sauce

MAKES 20 APPETIZERS

This sophisticated recipe is the creation of Barak Hirschowitz, a South African chef who was born in Israel, grew up in Cincinnati, started cooking in New York, and moved to Cape Town, where he has cooked for years. He has since left the kitchen to create South Africa Chef (www.sachef.com), a recruitment and staff-training program for South Africa's booming culinary and hospitality industry.

CHUTNEY

1 tablespoon olive oil

1 small onion, finely chopped

2 large Granny Smith apples, peeled, cored, and diced

1 tablespoon balsamic vinegar

2 tablespoons brown sugar

3 tablespoons peach-type chutney, such as Mrs. Ball's chutney

2 tablespoons whole-grain mustard

1 small red chile pepper, seeded and finely chopped

1 teaspoon chopped fresh mint

SAUCE

¼ cup passion fruit juice, or guava or pineapple juice

½ cup dry white wine

½ small onion, finely chopped

1 bay leaf

4 or 5 black peppercorns

½ cup heavy cream

2 tablespoons butter, chilled and diced

FRITTERS

2 to 3 cups lard, olive oil, or peanut oil, for frying

1 cup all-purpose flour, plus additional for dredging

1 egg

2 teaspoons salt

1 teaspoon freshly grated nutmeg

Milk

20 fresh oysters, shucked, shells reserved

4 ounces smoked trout or smoked Atlantic salmon, cut into 1-inch-wide slices

Ease of Preparation: Difficult

To make the chutney: Heat the olive oil in a medium pan over medium heat. Add the onion and cook slowly, stirring, until soft. Add all the remaining chutney ingredients and simmer for 10 to 15 minutes, until the apples are soft and most of the liquid has evaporated. Be careful not to let the mixture burn; if necessary, reduce the heat or move the pan off the heat for a minute or two. When the chutney is thick and soft, set aside and keep warm.

To make the sauce: Combine the passion fruit juice, wine, onion, bay leaf, and peppercorns in a small saucepan and cook over medium heat until the liquid has reduced by two-thirds. Add the cream and reduce again by two-thirds. Remove from the heat and strain the sauce into a bowl. Whisk in the butter until melted. Set the sauce aside and let it sit at room temperature.

To make the fritters: In a deep-sided pan, heat the lard or oil hot enough for deep frying. Meanwhile, mix all the batter ingredients together, adding just enough milk to thicken the batter for coating. Wrap each oyster in a strip of the trout, and dredge the wrapped oyster in flour, coating it all over. When the oil is hot enough for frying, slip the oysters carefully into the batter, a few at a time. Fry, turning, until golden brown. Remove with a slotted spoon to paper towels to drain, return the oil to frying temperature, and fry the remaining wrapped oysters in the same way.

To serve, place a small amount of warm chutney in the oyster shell. Place a fried oyster on the chutney and top with some of the passion fruit sauce. Serve.

NOTE: You can serve the fried oysters in other seafood shells, available at cookware stores.

PAIRING South African Chardonnay, with its combination of creamy toast and food-friendly minerality, will hold its own against the complex flavor profile of this dish; recommended producers include Hamilton Russell, De Wetshof, and Mulderbosch.

Lobster à l'Américaine with Basmati-Risotto Cakes

SERVES 4

Chef Didier Virot of Aix restaurant in New York City serves a traditional lobster à l'Américaine accompanied by crispy sautéed rice cakes. The rice cakes are breaded in panko, Japanese-style bread crumbs.

PAIRING Northern Rhône Marsanne, ideally Hermitage Blanc—a rich, full-bodied, moderately dry white with notes of spice, pear, orange and peach—has enough alcohol and complexity to take on the lobster, but effectively matches the fresher flavors here, too; recommended producers include J.L. Chave, E. Guigal, and Marc Sorrel.

LOBSTER AND SAUCE

3 lobsters

¼ cup plus 2 tablespoons olive oil

2 shallots, sliced

2 celery ribs, chopped

2 carrots, chopped

2 tablespoons tomato paste

¼ cup cognac

8 plum tomatoes, cut into quarters

1½ cups dry white wine

1 small bunch tarragon, chopped

3 large sprigs fresh rosemary

1 small bunch fresh flat-leaf parsley, stems reserved, leaves finely chopped

5 garlic cloves, chopped

¼ teaspoon cayenne pepper

½ teaspoon salt

Freshly ground black pepper

Fresh lemon juice

BASMATI-RISOTTO CAKES

1 cup basmati rice

½ teaspoon kosher salt

1 cup heavy cream

1 cup panko, or unseasoned dried bread crumbs

1 egg, beaten

1½ tablespoons unsalted butter

Ease of Preparation: Difficult to Very Difficult

To make the lobster and sauce: Cook the lobsters in a large pot of boiling water for 1½ to 2 minutes, then shock them under cold running water. Remove the meat from the lobsters and set aside. Chop the shells into chunks. Place the shells and ¼ cup olive oil in a large, heavy pot and sauté over high heat until they turn red. Reduce the heat to low and add the shallots, celery, carrots, and tomato paste. Cook, covered, for about 10 minutes, stirring occasionally. Add the cognac and continue to cook, covered, for another 5 minutes.

Combine the tomatoes and white wine in a food processor and purée. Transfer the tomato mixture to the pot, along with 1 cup water, half of the chopped tarragon, rosemary sprigs, parsley stems, and garlic. Season with cayenne, salt, and pepper. Cover and let simmer very slowly for 30 minutes, stirring every 10 minutes.

Strain the mixture through a colander with large holes, pressing down on the solids to extract as much liquid as possible; discard solids in the colander. Strain the mixture again through a fine sieve. The consistency of the sauce should be thick enough to coat a spoon. (If the sauce seems too thin, place it in a small saucepan and simmer to reduce it to the desired consistency.) Add the remaining tarragon, all but 1 tablespoon of the chopped parsley leaves, and the lemon juice. Taste and adjust the seasoning as necessary.

To make the basmati-risotto cakes: Line an 11 x 7-inch baking pan with waxed paper.

Combine the rice, salt, and 1 cup water in a saucepan over medium heat. Cover and cook until the rice is almost tender, about 14 minutes. Stir in the cream and cook until the liquid is absorbed, about 5 minutes longer. Taste and add more salt, if necessary. Spread the mixture in the prepared pan, about ½-inch thick, and let cool. Refrigerate until thoroughly chilled, about 2 hours.

Finely grind the panko in a food processor and pour into a shallow dish. Using a knife or large cookie cutter, cut the rice into 8 round, 2- to 3-inch cakes. Carefully brush both sides of the rice cakes with egg, then dip them into the panko to coat on both sides.

Melt the butter in a nonstick skillet over medium heat. Fry the rice cakes, without crowding the pan, until crispy, about 3 to 4 minutes per side, until golden. Take care when you flip them so they don't break apart.

Just before serving, warm the remaining 2 tablespoons olive oil in a large skillet over high heat. Season the lobster meat with salt and pepper and add it to the hot oil. Sauté for 3 to 5 minutes until the lobster is cooked through, opaque and just slightly firm. Toss the lobster with the the sauce and sprinkle with reserved parsley.

To serve, divide the lobster among 4 shallow bowls and garnish each with two basmati-risotto cakes.

Dungeness Crab Salad with Roasted Beets, Arugula, and Blood Orange Vinaigrette

SERVES 4

This recipe originally appeared in *Wine Enthusiast* courtesy of Chef Jerry Regester of The Restaurant at Wente Vineyards in Livermore, California. The fresh-tasting, colorful combination capitalizes on several of the best foods that the West Coast has to offer: California produce and Pacific Dungeness crab.

BLOOD ORANGE VINAIGRETTE

2 blood oranges

1 tablespoon grated fresh ginger

1 tablespoon honey

Salt and freshly ground black pepper

1 cup extra virgin olive oil

SALAD

3 whole beets, greens removed

3 tablespoons white wine vinegar

Salt and freshly ground black pepper

2 blood oranges

8 ounces Dungeness crabmeat, picked over

Blood orange vinaigrette (see above)

1 cup arugula

1 bunch chives, chopped

Ease of Preparation: Moderate

To make the vinaigrette: Juice the oranges and put the juice into a nonreactive medium bowl. Add the ginger, honey, and a pinch of salt and pepper, then slowly drizzle in the olive oil while whisking. Set aside until ready to use.

Preheat the oven to 325°F.

To make the salad: In a small baking dish, toss the beets with the vinegar, a pinch of salt and pepper, and a splash of water, then cover tightly with foil and roast until tender, at least 30 minutes for small beets and about an hour for larger beets. Let the beets cool, then peel and slice them medium-thick. In a medium bowl, toss the beet slices with a splash of the vinaigrette; set aside.

Peel the oranges and cut them into segments. In a large bowl, combine the orange segments and crab, and toss with some of the vinaigrette.

To serve, arrange arugula in the middle of four plates, top with the crab salad, then garnish each plate with beets and orange segments. Sprinkle the chives over each salad and serve.

> **PAIRING** A domestic white blend known as Meritage (usually containing Sauvignon Blanc and Semillon, among other grapes) offers both crispness and complexity to match the lively citrus and rich crab in this dish; recommended producers include Murrieta's Well and M. Cosentino from California, and Three Rivers from Washington.

Confit of Tuna with Onion Confit, Endive Salad, and Sauce Verte

SERVES 4

This recipe is adapted from *The Farallon Cookbook* by Mark Franz and Lisa Weiss. The dish is a play on the concept of *confit*, which is traditionally meat or poultry cooked in its own fat. Here, tuna is cooked in olive oil, and the onion confit is slow-cooked in butter.

ONION CONFIT

5 tablespoons unsalted butter

1 bay leaf

5 juniper berries, lightly crushed

3 large yellow onions, each cut into 8 wedges

¾ cup dry red wine

Kosher salt and freshly ground black pepper

TUNA CONFIT

2 tablespoons cardamom pods

4 (5-ounce) tuna fillets, 1½- to 2-inches thick

Kosher salt and freshly ground black pepper

3 to 4 cups olive oil

LEMON VINAIGRETTE

1 tablespoon fresh lemon juice

¼ cup extra virgin olive oil

Kosher salt and freshly ground black pepper

SAUCE VERTE

1 garlic clove, smashed

1 tablespoon fresh tarragon leaves

1 tablespoon fresh thyme leaves

2 teaspoons salt-packed capers, rinsed, or vinegar-brined capers, drained

3 anchovy fillets, drained

3 tablespoons coarsely chopped fresh chives

¼ cup fresh basil leaves

¼ cup fresh flat-leaf parsley leaves

¼ teaspoon freshly ground black pepper

½ teaspoon green peppercorns, drained

½ teaspoon fresh lemon juice

¼ cup fresh orange juice

1 teaspoon Champagne vinegar

¼ cup olive oil

Kosher salt

ENDIVE SALAD

4 heads Belgian endive, cored and cut into thin diagonal strips

½ cup watercress leaves

Ease of Preparation: Difficult

To make the onion confit: In a small saucepan, melt the butter with the bay leaf and juniper berries over medium-low heat. Add the onions and cook, stirring, until soft, about 15 minutes. Add the wine and season with salt and pepper. Cover and cook for about 30 minutes. Uncover and cook to reduce wine until syrupy, about 15 minutes. Cover and keep warm until ready to serve or refrigerate for up to 2 days.

To make the tuna confit: In a small, dry pan, roast the cardamom pods over medium heat for 3 to 4 minutes. Let cool. Remove the seeds from the pods and coarsely grind the seeds in a mortar. Sprinkle the tuna with salt and pepper to taste and the cardamom. Put the seasoned tuna into a medium saucepan and add olive oil to cover by at least ½ inch. Over high heat, bring the oil to 180°F. Remove from the heat, cover, and let sit for 5 to 10 minutes, depending on the desired doneness. Using a slotted spoon, transfer the tuna to a plate. Strain and reserve the oil for another use.

To make the lemon vinaigrette: In a small bowl, whisk the lemon juice and olive oil to blend. Season with salt and pepper. Set the vinaigrette aside until ready to serve or cover and refrigerate for up to 1 day.

To make the sauce verte: Combine the garlic, tarragon, thyme, capers, anchovies, chives, basil, parsley, pepper, green peppercorns, lemon juice, orange juice, and Champagne vinegar in a food processor and purée, scraping down the sides of the container once or twice. With the machine running, gradually add the olive oil and purée until the sauce reaches the consistency of thick mayonnaise. If it's too thick, add a little water to thin. Season with salt. Transfer to another container or bowl, cover, and set aside. Refrigerate the sauce for up to 4 hours.

To make the salad: In a large bowl, toss the endive and watercress with the lemon vinaigrette.

To serve, place a pool of sauce verte on each of 4 serving plates. Place a tuna fillet on one side of the sauce and spoon one-fourth of the onions on the other side of the sauce. Place equal portions of the salad on top of the tuna and onions so that it falls slightly to the side. Serve immediately.

NOTE: If you wish, the tuna confit can be made 1 day ahead and refrigerated; bring it to room temperature before serving. The onion confit can be made up to 2 days ahead and kept in the refrigerator. Toss the salad with the vinaigrette just before serving.

NEVER SAY NEVER **PAIRING**

With its floral fruitiness, Viognier from Condrieu in France, or a domestic Viognier from California or Washington softens the crispness of tuna, lemon, and vinegar here. Recommended Condrieu producers include E. Guigal, Delas Frères, and Les Vins de Vienne; recommended domestic producers include Alban from California's Central Coast and Cayuse from Washington.

About Rich, Full-Bodied White Wines

The varieties of wines covered in this chapter are few, but make spectacular choices. Chardonnay is at the head of the class, and over the past 30 years, the Burgundy blueprint of barrel fermentation and oak aging has been adopted in many countries and locales, including the entire west coast of the United States, Italy, Australia and New Zealand, South Africa, and Argentina and Chile.

What makes Chardonnay the leading varietal for this style of wine is that it takes to barrel fermentation and oak aging better than almost any other white grape. Chardonnay ripens slightly later than most white grapes, and thus it arrives at the crush pad with the natural corpulence and lofty alcohol capable of standing up to the resins, tannins, aromas, and flavors imparted by new oak barrels.

But Chardonnay is not alone in this field. In Bordeaux, Sauvignon Blanc is commonly blended with naturally hefty Sémillon grapes and then aged in oak. In addition, a select group of Loire Valley vintners, whose natural product is Sauvignon Blanc, employs partial barrel fermentation and aging in used oak barrels. And in France's Rhône Valley, grapes including Marsanne and Roussanne are made much in the Chardonnay style, with barrel aging resulting in gold-tinted wines of richness and complexity. Viognier, another French variety with Rhône roots, also yields big, floral wines with high alcohol levels and plenty of mouthfeel.

It should come as no surprise that rich, opulent foods go best with rich, full-bodied white wines. The pairing of Le Montrachet—the world's most expensive and sought-after white Burgundy—with butter-poached lobster is widely regarded as a dream meal fit for royalty. But enjoying a broiled Maine lobster with a lesser Burgundy or a Chardonnay from California or Australia should not leave anyone feeling deprived.

When pouring rich, full-bodied white wines with food, serve similarly indulgent foods. The aforementioned lobster, along with Dungeness crabs, Florida Stone crabs, sea urchin, scallops, and caviar are excellent starting points for building a meal. White truffles and white truffle oil are also recommended if you're pouring a full-tilt white wine, as are more humble but still rich ingredients, such as corn, squash, and potatoes. With big wines, shoot for big pairings. It's the best way to go.

Chapter 3

Rosés & Light Red Wines

In a traditional cookbook, you would find the recipes we have paired with rosé and light red wines scattered throughout several chapters. But rosé and light red wines are so food-friendly, especially with today's relaxed style of eating, we have collected them in one place. For three of the six recipes in this chapter, relaxed and easy-to-make (and enjoy) are the operative descriptors: You will find a French vegetable soup, a breezy American summer salad, and another French classic, *pan bagnat*, Nice's renowned tuna-and-olive sandwich on a baguette. The recipes share an enviable informality. Each is appropriate for lunch or an early or late supper; each relies on ingredients that are available, and each teams up with a wine that is not exacting or fancy, just pleasurable, like the food it accompanies.

The remaining three recipes—bouillabaisse, a sushi-style tuna napoleon, and Moroccan-style lamb shanks—demonstrate just how versatile rosé or light red wine can be when it comes to pairing it with food. These dishes are sophisticated by comparison to the easy-going soup/salad/sandwich lot. That, and still the pairing of choice is a rosé or a light red. The point: Rosé and light red wines are inclusive, inviting, and surprisingly adaptive when it comes to pairing with different kinds of foods. How might we describe that state of events? In a word, rosy.

Summer Tomato Salad

SERVES 4 TO 6

For this simple salad or one of its variations (see the suggestions below), look for the best, vine-ripened tomatoes you can find at your local farmers' market—or perhaps over your backyard fence, if you don't have them in your own garden.

6 medium or large slicing tomatoes

5 small tomatoes, about 1½ inches in diameter

2 cups small cherry tomatoes

2 small red torpedo onions, thinly sliced

Kosher salt

6 ounces fresh mozzarella cheese, thinly sliced

6 garlic cloves, minced

Kosher salt, Sel gris, or other solar-dried sea salt

¼ cup best-quality extra virgin olive oil

Freshly ground black pepper

Fresh basil leaves

Basil flowers, for garnish (optional)

Ease of Preparation: Easy

Slice off and discard the stem and blossom ends of the slicing tomatoes and cut the tomatoes into ⅜-inch-thick slices. Set aside. Cut the small tomatoes (through the poles, not the equator) into wedges and set aside. Cut the cherry tomatoes in half, cutting pear-shaped tomatoes through the poles and round tomatoes through the equator; set them aside.

On a large platter, assemble the salad: begin by arranging a circle of large tomato slices on the outside edge of the plate, alternating colors and overlapping the slices slightly. Next, add a ring of onion slices, overlapping the onions onto the tomatoes by half. Add another ring of tomatoes, moving towards the center, and another of onions. In the center of the plate, arrange a circle of small tomato wedges. Tuck slices of mozzarella here and there. Arrange the remaining tomato wedges on top of the sliced tomatoes and scatter the sliced cherry tomatoes and the garlic over the salad. Season with salt and let sit for 15 minutes.

Drizzle the olive oil over the salad. Add several turns of black pepper and a light sprinkling of salt. Garnish with basil leaves and basil flowers, if desired. Serve immediately, or cover and serve within 1 hour.

Variations:

- Scatter 2 cups poached salt cod over the salad before adding the olive oil.

- Scatter Italian canned tuna (drained) over the salad before adding the olive oil.

- Omit the fresh mozzarella and crumble 4 ounces blue cheese or goat cheese over the salad before adding the olive oil.

- Use sweet onions (Maui, Walla Walla, or Vidalia) instead of the torpedo onions.

- Omit the basil; scatter 1 or 2 minced serrano chiles and 2 tablespoons minced fresh cilantro over the salad before adding the olive oil.

- Fry 6 rashers of bacon until crisp; crumble and scatter the bacon over the salad just before serving.

Tuna and Hard-Boiled Egg Salad on a Baguette

Pan Bagnat

SERVES 4 TO 6

A specialty of the French Riviera city of Nice, this sandwich was devised as a clever use for stale bread. Pan bagnat means "bathed bread" and indeed the bread absorbs the olive oil, vinegar, and tomato and anchovy juices nicely, creating an innovative, edible treat. If you choose to substitute a ciabatta loaf for the baguette, there is no need to remove the interior. To save time, you can use purchased olive tapenade instead of making your own.

TAPENADE

1 cup pitted kalamata or niçoise olives

2 tablespoons olive oil

2 anchovy fillets

1 teaspoon vinegar-brined capers, drained

1 small garlic clove

SANDWICHES

2 (6-ounce) cans oil-packed tuna, drained

2 eggs, hard-boiled, peeled, and chopped

⅔ cup diced tomato or quartered grape tomatoes

⅔ cup diced peeled cucumber

½ cup chopped red onion

2 tablespoons extra virgin olive oil

1 tablespoon red wine vinegar

Salt and freshly ground black pepper

1 baguette, split lengthwise, or 1 ciabatta of equal size

Mixed salad greens

Ease of Preparation: Easy

To make the tapenade: Combine all ingredients in a food processor and blend until smooth.

To assemble the sandwiches: In a medium bowl, combine the tuna, eggs, tomato, cucumber, onion, olive oil, and vinegar. Season with salt and pepper.

Hollow out the cut sides of the baguette by removing some of the bread with your fingers and discard. Spread the tapenade on the cut sides. (Refrigerate any unused tapenade in a covered container; it will keep for up to several weeks.) Spoon the tuna mixture onto the bottom half of the baguette, pressing to make it adhere. Top with the salad greens. Place the other half of the baguette on top. Wrap the sandwich securely in plastic wrap and refrigerate until ready to serve.

To pack for a picnic: Before wrapping the finished sandwich in plastic, cut it into four to six pieces; reassemble the filled loaf and wrap securely, first in plastic wrap and then in aluminum foil. Place in an ice chest protected from direct contact with melting ice.

To serve, remove the sandwich from the refrigerator (or cooler) about 1 hour before serving to bring to room temperature. Unwrap just before serving.

PAIRING

PAIRING The bone-dry crispness of a Tavel rosé is a
perfect accompaniment to the tuna, onion, and vinegar
in this dish; recommended producers include Château
d'Aqueria; Les Vignerons de Tavel, and Brotte. A domestic alternative would be one of the many "vin gris," such
as Saintsbury's Vin Gris of Pinot Noir.

Vegetable Soup with Pistou

Provençal Soupe au Pistou

SERVES 4

Pistou—pesto's French cousin—is a versatile and prized condiment. Here, it elevates a simple vegetable minestrone to a dish with amazing taste and intensity. This version of the recipe is from the Restaurant Galerie des Arcades in Biot, a tiny hilltop hamlet near Antibes on the Côte d'Azur.

SOUP

2 cups dried flageolet beans, or white or navy beans

1 celery rib, chopped

2 zucchini, cubed

2 potatoes, cubed

1 onion, chopped

Salt

PISTOU

1 large bunch fresh basil, stemmed

2 or 3 garlic cloves

1 tomato, seeded and finely chopped

¼ cup olive oil

GARNISH

Olive oil

Freshly grated Parmesan cheese, preferably Parmigiano-Reggiano

Ease of Preparation: Moderate

To make the soup: Place the beans in a large bowl or pot and add enough water to cover. Let the beans soak overnight. Transfer the beans with their soaking liquid to a large pot, add more water if necessary to cover, and bring to a boil. Reduce heat and simmer for 20 minutes. Drain the beans and set aside.

Place the celery, zucchini, potatoes, onion, and salt to taste in a large pot. Add enough water to cover and bring to a boil, then reduce the heat and let simmer for 1½ hours. Add the drained beans.

To make the *pistou*: Combine the basil leaves, garlic, tomato, and olive oil in a blender and chop finely until it becomes a syrupy paste.

To serve, ladle the soup into large soup bowls, then dab a generous spoonful of *pistou* on top of the soup, stirring it in with a spoon. Drizzle olive oil over each serving and sprinkle grated Parmesan cheese on top. Serve additional Parmesan at the table, if desired.

NOTE: Some versions of this recipe call for a handful of cooked cubes or crumbles of smoked bacon for extra flavor; add with the beans.

> **PAIRING** The lively pink grapefruit and red fruit notes of a Côtes de Provençe rosé will enhance the freshness and light flavors of this beloved traditional dish; recommended producers include Domaines Ott, Mas de Gourgonnier, and Château Peyrassol. A rosé from the Côtes du Rhône would also work.

Vintner Grill's Bouillabaisse

SERVES 2

Created by Executive Chef Matthew Silverman of Las Vegas's Vintner Grill, this classic and lively seafood entrée is ideal for an al fresco summer supper.

2 tablespoons olive oil

1 tablespoon minced garlic

2 tablespoons minced shallot

2 tablespoons chopped fennel

¾ cup dry white wine

1 lemon

6 ounces snapper fillet, skinned

10 fresh mussels

¼ pound scallops, halved

6 shrimp

1 cup tomato broth (see Note)

4 tablespoons butter

Salt and freshly ground black pepper

Sugar to taste

4 teaspoons chopped fresh flat-leaf parsley

6 ounces calamari, cleaned and cut into bite-sized rings

2 teaspoons extra virgin olive oil, for finishing

2 French baguettes, sliced and toasted

Ease of Preparation: Moderate

Preheat a large sauté pan over medium heat. Put the olive oil in the warm sauté pan. Add the garlic, shallot, and fennel and cook over medium heat until the vegetables have softened (do not allow to brown), about 5 to 10 minutes. Add the wine and a squeeze of lemon and deglaze the pan.

Add the snapper, mussels, scallops, shrimp, and tomato broth. (*Note*: It is important to add the seafood in the order listed so that none of it overcooks.) Bring to a simmer. Add the butter and cook until melted and combined. Gently stir the mixture and if there are any mussels that have not opened, discard them. Season with salt, pepper, and sugar. Add 2 teaspoons of the chopped parsley.

Add the calamari just before the dish is finished cooking and cook until it is opaque and slightly firm.

Using a slotted spoon, heap the fish and shellfish in the bottom of 2 soup bowls, piling the seafood high. Pour the broth over the seafood. Top with the remaining chopped parsley, then drizzle 1 teaspoon of the olive oil over each serving. Garnish with the toasted baguette and serve immediately.

NOTE: Before cooking the bouillabaisse, you will need to make the tomato broth. In a nonreactive saucepan, heat 1 tablespoon olive oil until it ripples, then add 1 small chopped onion and cook, stirring, until it is soft and translucent. Add 3 ripe tomatoes and their juice, ½ cup dry white wine, and the leaves of 2 sprigs fresh thyme, and cook, stirring occasionally, for 10 to 15 minutes, until the tomatoes have turned to mush and the alcohol has cooked off. Strain the liquid into a heatproof measuring cup and process the solids in a food processor until smooth. Add enough of the purée to the strained broth to make 1 cup tomato broth.

PAIRING Light and energetic but with some red fruit structure to add complexity, a Provençal or Spanish rosé will complement the crisp seafood flavors as well as the earthier, herbal elements of the soup; recommended appellations include Côtes de Provençe and Bandol in France, and Rioja, Navarra and Empordà-Costa Brava in Spain.

Tuna "alla Napoletana" with Osetra Caviar

SERVES 2

This tuna tartare-style starter, courtesy of Chef Chris Manning of Etoile at Domaine Chandon in Yountville, California, calls for the freshest, grade-A ahi tuna possible.

TUNA TARTARE

4 ounces tuna (grade-A ahi), diced

1 tablespoon chopped chives

3 tablespoons extra virgin olive oil

Sea salt

White pepper

4 ounces Roma tomato, peeled, seeded, and diced

1 ¼ teaspoons fresh lemon juice

¼ cup zucchini, rinsed and diced very small

LEMON CREAM

¼ cup heavy cream

2 teaspoons fresh lemon juice

Salt

ASSEMBLY

1 ounce osetra caviar

2 tablespoons lemon zest, dried

Chives, for garnish (optional)

Crisp crackers, for serving

Ease of Preparation: Moderate

To make the tuna tartare: Combine the tuna, chives, 1 tablespoon of the olive oil, and salt and pepper to taste in a bowl and mix well.

In another bowl, combine the tomato, 1 teaspoon of the lemon juice, 1 tablespoon of the olive oil and salt and pepper to taste; mix well.

Combine the zucchini, the remaining ¼ teaspoon lemon juice and 1 tablespoon olive oil, and salt and pepper to taste in a small bowl and mix well.

To make the lemon cream: In a stainless steel bowl, whisk the cream until stiff, fold in the lemon juice, and season with salt.

To assemble: Place a 5-inch circular mold in the center of a serving plate. Fill the mold with half of the tomato salad; top with half of the zucchini salad, and finally half of the tuna tartare. Remove the ring mold, dollop with lemon cream, and top with caviar. Repeat with remaining half of ingredients to make one more. Sprinkle the plates with lemon zest and garnish them with whole chives, if desired. Serve at once with thin crisp crackers.

> **PAIRING** The elegant but upfront flavors of this dish call for a wine that is both delicate and assertive, like a Sangiovese-based rosé; recommended producers include Solo Rosa and Iron Horse from California, Barnard Griffin from Washington, and Castello di Ama from Italy.

Moroccan-Style Lamb Shanks with Olives and Preserved Lemons

SERVES 4

Few cuisines have lamb dishes as delicious as those that come from Morocco. Because nearly all stews improve with time, you can prepare this dish the day before serving it. For convenience, you can marinate the shanks overnight before cooking them. Steamed couscous is a very good choice with this dish, as is barley, farro, and the small round pasta known as *acini di pepe*. Preserved lemons (lemons that have been brined in a salt-lemon juice) are sold at some specialty foods stores and at markets that feature North African products.

4 garlic cloves, crushed, plus 6 garlic cloves, minced

Kosher salt

2 teaspoons paprika

2 teaspoons ground cumin

2 teaspoons ground coriander

1 teaspoon grated fresh ginger

Freshly ground black pepper

4 lamb shanks, trimmed of outer fat

3 tablespoons olive oil

2 yellow onions, diced

¾ cup green olives, pitted and sliced

4 preserved lemon wedges, slivered

4 preserved lemon wedges, for garnish

Ease of Preparation: Moderate

Put the crushed garlic cloves in a mortar, and add 1 teaspoon salt. Use a wooden pestle to grind the garlic to a paste. Stir in the paprika, cumin, coriander, and ginger, and several turns of black pepper. Rub some of the mixture over each lamb shank and set on a baking sheet. Cover the shanks and refrigerate for several hours or overnight.

Preheat the oven to 300°F.

Pour the olive oil into a large deep pan set over medium heat. Add the lamb shanks and brown them evenly on all sides. Using tongs, transfer the shanks to a plate or baking sheet. Add the onions to the pan, season with several pinches of salt, and cook until they are soft and fragrant, about 15 minutes. Do not let the onions brown. Add the minced garlic and sauté 2 minutes more.

Set the browned shanks on top of the onions and garlic, add 2 cups water, cover the pan, and set on the middle rack of the oven. Bake the shanks until the lamb falls off the bone, about 2½ hours. Check occasionally and add more water if needed. Uncover the pot for the final 20 minutes of cooking. Remove from the oven, cover, and let rest for up to 30 minutes.

To serve, transfer the lamb shanks to a platter. Set the pan over a burner. If there is a lot of liquid left, cook over medium-high heat until it is reduced to about ½ cup. Stir in the sliced olives and slivered preserved lemon wedges; pour the sauce over the shanks. Garnish with the remaining wedges of preserved lemons. Serve immediately.

PAIRING A Cru Beaujolais, which offers more heft than the simply light, fruity flavors of a regular Beaujolais, has the kind of red juicy fruit and acidity that will pair nicely with the spice and citrus in this entrée; recommended communes include Morgon, Fleurie, Juliénas, and St.-Amour.

About Rosés and Light Red Wines

As in the worlds of fashion, film, music, and automobiles, trends in the wine world come and go. And by all measures, we seem to be witnessing the start of the glory years for rosé.

Whereas dry rosé (which should not to be confused with the 1980s-era American concoction called White Zinfandel) was long a well-kept Mediterranean secret, word has gotten out that dry rosé wines are not only nice to look at, but also easy to drink. And guess what? They are incredibly food-friendly as well.

But first, let's define what rosé *is* by setting the record straight about what *it isn't*: rosé is not the result of mixing red and white wines to make a pink one. This is simply untrue. The overwhelming majority of rosé wines are based entirely on red grapes, the wines made by allowing the juice of the grapes to mix with the skins for a short period of time. (The skins are then removed prior to fermentation.) A touch of color is all that remains when the yeast is introduced to the juice and fermentation begins.

Grapes like Grenache, Syrah, Mourvèdre, and Tempranillo make some of the best and cleanest rosés, while you may also find rosé wines made from Cabernet Sauvignon, Merlot, Malbec, Sangiovese and other more obscure varietals. Like aromatic white wines, dry rosé wines are at their best in the year following the date of their vintage. Any rosé more than two years old should be avoided.

As for light red wines, think Beaujolais (made from the Gamay grape), Dolcetto, and certain wines hailing from the southern Rhône valley, i.e., Côtes-du-Rhône and the occasional lighter-framed Grenache-based wines from the commune of Gigondas. The hallmarks of these wines are their zesty acidity and mild, fleshy tannins. Which isn't to say that Côtes-du-Rhône, which is the name of a sprawling appellation and not a single grape type, can't be the source of bigger wines that might be better categorized as fruit-forward and medium-bodied.

When it comes to matching food with rosés and light red wines, a good rule of thumb is to pair a region's recipes with its wines: southern French specialties like salade niçoise, pissaladière (a sort of Mediterranean pizza), bouillabaisse, and grilled seafood almost demand a dry Provençal rosé, while heartier dishes like Italian cold cuts, roast leg of lamb, and couscous with chicken or spicy merguez sausages cry out for a fresh, lively red, such as a Beaujolais, Dolcetto, or Côtes-du-Rhône.

Chapter 4

Medium-Bodied, Fruit-Forward Red Wines

If you are in the mood for a tomato or potato salad, a simple, comforting soup, or Provence's famous *pan bagnat*, don't look for them in this chapter. (For those everyday favorites, go to Chapter 3—Rosés and Light Red Wines, instead.) The reason? The dishes that seem to pair best with this "step up," or progression, to medium-bodied, fruit-forward red wines have something else in common: a heightened gravitas. In short, the dishes themselves are less informal. Unlike the previous chapter, no finger foods or snacks follow. Entrées star here.

And they are entrées with significant flavor—assertive flavor—that range in complexity from portobello mushrooms to olives, duck, and lamb, prepared in a variety of appealing ways. And just as there is nothing shy about the range of flavors and ingredients in this group of recipes, the types of dishes themselves are more complex than those in the Rosés and Light Red Wines chapter. Here, you will find substantial, hearty fare suitable for a chilly fall or winter evening. In sum, what we have in the pages that follow is a mutual admiration society—dishes of substance paired with wines of commensurate bearing.

Among the main courses, if lamb is to your liking, you have an international *carte* from which to choose: from India, *sali bota* (lamb with apricots); from Aleppo (Syria), lamb skewers with grilled cherries; from India via China, lamb ribs with exotic red rice; and from Greece, a one-of-a-kind moussaka, with layers of vegetables and meat blanketed in a Greek yogurt-béchamel sauce.

There are tempting seafood entrées, too, including an intriguing spicy Mexican shrimp stew and a Mediterranean-inspired grilled salmon with olive butter, each paired with a red. Seafood and red wine? It's a combination that we now know can work brilliantly. Which brings us to the most surprising match-up of all: asparagus dressed with balsamic vinegar and paired with a Tuscan Sangiovese.

Perfect Portobello and Red Pepper Almost Burgers

SERVES 4

Even those who don't eat meat crave a "meaty" burger now and then. This recipe treats the portobello mushroom (really an overgrown cremini mushroom) as if it were a chunk of ground sirloin. If properly prepared, there is a chance that, with your eyes closed, you might not be able to tell the difference.

MAYONNAISE

1 cup purchased (jarred) roasted red peppers, drained and coarsely chopped

¼ cup mayonnaise

1 garlic clove, chopped

1 tablespoon Tabasco sauce

Salt and freshly ground black pepper

BURGERS

4 large portobello mushrooms, stems removed, wiped clean

1 sweet onion, such as Vidalia, thickly sliced

1 tablespoon vegetable oil

Salt and freshly ground black pepper

4 whole wheat hamburger buns, split in half

1 bunch arugula, trimmed, rinsed, and patted dry

Ease of Preparation: Easy

Start a charcoal grill and build a medium-hot fire, or preheat a gas grill to medium-high, or preheat a broiler, setting the rack on the second-highest level.

To make the red pepper mayonnaise: Blend the peppers, mayonnaise, garlic, and Tabasco sauce in a food processor fitted with the steel blade until smooth. Season the mayonnaise with salt and pepper to taste and chill until ready to use.

To prepare the portobello mushrooms: Brush the mushrooms and onion slices with the oil and sprinkle with salt and pepper. Grill the mushrooms and onions until tender, turning often, about 10 minutes.

To serve, arrange 1 grilled portobello, gill-side down, on the bottom half of each split bun. Top with some of the grilled onions, a generous tablespoon of the red pepper mayonnaise, and arugula leaves. Set the remaining bun halves on top, and serve immediately, with the remaining red pepper mayonnaise as an accompaniment.

> **PAIRING** The earthy overtones of Carneros Pinot Noir match the forest floor flavors of these burgers; recommended producers include Etude, Beringer, and Saintsbury.

Pork Chops with Pinot Noir and Espresso Demi-Glace

SERVES 6

Demi-glace, a rich, stock-based glaze, adds considerable flavor to this recipe, but making it from scratch would add more time than most of us have to spend on one dish. It's so much easier to purchase demi-glace ready-to-use in the refrigerated or freezer section of a well-stocked specialty foods store. The chops need to marinate at least four hours before grilling.

½ cup olive oil

½ cup chopped fresh thyme

1 tablespoon chopped garlic

2 tablespoons chopped shallots

1 tablespoon Dijon mustard

6 (6- to 8-ounce) center-cut pork chops

½ cup Pinot Noir

2 cups pork or veal demi-glace

¼ cup espresso

1 tablespoon vinegar

Ease of Preparation: Easy

In a medium bowl, whisk the olive oil, thyme, garlic, shallots, and mustard together until the marinade is well combined. Place the pork chops in a shallow pan and pour the marinade over. Cover the pan and let the chops marinate in the refrigerator for 4 to 8 hours.

Heat a grill (outdoor or stovetop) over medium-high heat. Remove the pork chops from the marinade and discard the marinade. Arrange the chops on the preheated grill and cook for 4 to 8 minutes per side, to the desired degree of doneness. (If the chops are boneless, they will take less time to cook.)

Meanwhile, make the sauce: In a medium saucepan, reduce the wine over medium heat by half. Stir in the demi-glace, espresso, and vinegar and bring the mixture to a simmer. Remove the pan from the heat.

To serve, place the pork chops on a serving platter and pour the sauce over them.

> **PAIRING** The liveliness of an Oregon Pinot Noir will offset the richness of the demi-glace; recommended producers include Ken Wright, Ponzi, and Hamacher.

Wild Rice Salad with Mushrooms, Cranberries, and Walnut Oil

SERVES 6

Chef Alfred Portale of the Gotham Bar and Grill in New York City created this easy-to-make but elegant side dish. Paired with a duck breast or roasted turkey, it makes for a delicious winter holiday bite.

GRAINS

1 teaspoon salt

1 cup wild rice

½ cup wheat berries (see Note)

SALAD

½ cup dried cranberries, coarsely chopped

1 tablespoon canola oil, or other neutral-flavored oil

1 ½ cups coarsely chopped portobello mushrooms

½ teaspoon salt

1 cup coarsely chopped walnuts, toasted

2 shallots, finely chopped

1 tablespoon chopped flat-leaf parsley

1 tablespoon walnut oil, or good-quality extra virgin olive oil

Freshly ground black pepper

Ease of Preparation: Easy

To cook the grains: Fill a large saucepan with 3 cups water and ½ teaspoon of the salt. In another large saucepan, add 3 cups water and remaining ½ teaspoon of the salt; bring both to a boil over high heat. Add the rice to the first saucepan and the wheat berries to the second; cover both, and reduce the heat to medium. Simmer, stirring occasionally. The rice should take about 40 to 50 minutes, and the wheat berries about 1 hour and 45 minutes. Drain if necessary and let cool slightly.

To make the salad: Place the cranberries in a small bowl, cover with 2 tablespoons of warm water, and set aside to soften, about 10 minutes. Drain.

In a small skillet, warm the oil over medium heat. Add the mushrooms and ½ teaspoon salt and sauté for 8 to 10 minutes. Let cool slightly before transferring to a serving bowl; add the walnuts, shallots, parsley, and softened cranberries. Add the cooled grains. Toss gently to combine. Drizzle the mixture with the walnut oil and season with pepper to taste. Serve the salad warm or at room temperature.

NOTE: The wheat berries will cook in about half the time if they are first soaked in water to cover overnight, preferably in the refrigerator.

> **PAIRING** The crisp acidity of a Loire Valley Cabernet Franc and its red fruit flavors will echo the cranberry flavors in this dish; recommended communes include Saumur-Champigny, Chinon, and Bourgueil. If these are difficult to find in your local shop, a Beaujolais makes a solid stand-in.

Lamb and Cherry Kebabs from Aleppo

MAKES 10 SKEWERS

This recipe is adapted from *Little Foods of the Mediterranean* by Clifford A. Wright. The spice blend, *baharat*, is a necessary ingredient, but you can easily make it yourself. The amounts given for each spice below will yield far more than the 2 tablespoons baharat needed, but the blend will keep for several months. If you use wooden skewers, be sure to soak them in water for about half an hour prior to assembly.

BAHARAT

¼ cup black peppercorns

¼ cup allspice berries

2 teaspoons ground cinnamon

1 teaspoon freshly grated nutmeg

KEBABS

1 ½ pounds boneless leg of lamb, trimmed of fat and cut into ½-inch cubes

2 tablespoons baharat (see above)

½ teaspoon freshly ground cumin seeds

½ teaspoon freshly ground coriander seeds

¼ teaspoon ground cinnamon

Salt and freshly ground black pepper

50 fresh black or Bing cherries, pitted

Pita bread

Tomato wedges

Pitted black olives

SPECIAL EQUIPMENT: **10 (8- to 10-inch) metal skewers, or wooden skewers soaked in water for 30 minutes**

Ease of Preparation: Moderate

To make the *baharat*: In a spice grinder or clean coffee mill, grind the peppercorns and allspice together; transfer to a bowl, and blend with the cinnamon and nutmeg. Store in a jar in your spice rack, away from sunlight. The spice blend will lose pungency as time goes by, but properly stored, it will be good for many months.

To make the kebabs: In a medium bowl, toss the lamb, baharat, cumin, coriander, cinnamon, salt, and pepper together. Cover with plastic wrap and refrigerate for 2 hours.

Meanwhile, prepare a hot charcoal fire or preheat a gas grill for 15 minutes on high heat.

Skewer the lamb, interspersed with the cherries. Place the skewers on the grill and cook, turning occasionally, until the meat is browned and springy to the touch, about 15 minutes. Serve immediately on a platter with pita bread, tomato wedges, and black olives.

PAIRING The structure and acidity of a Greek Agiorgitiko or Xinomavro will hold its own against the heady spice and sweetness of this dish; recommended producers include Biblia Chora, Boutari, Kyr-Yianni, and Tsantali.

Grilled Salmon with Olive Butter and Orzo

SERVES 4

Olive butter is an excellent way to infuse a dish with rich flavor. You can make it ahead and keep it chilled for up to five days. It's wonderful with this grilled salmon dish, but you'll find other uses for it as well.

OLIVE BUTTER

1 garlic clove, crushed

1 small shallot, peeled

About 18 oil-cured olives, pitted

1 tablespoon chopped fresh flat-leaf parsley

½ cup (1 stick) unsalted butter, at room temperature

2 teaspoons Dijon mustard

Freshly ground black pepper

Kosher salt

SALMON

Kosher salt

6 ounces orzo, acini di pepe, or other small, seed-shaped pasta

1 medium (about 2 pounds) wild king salmon fillet, scaled and cut into 4 pieces of equal weight

Freshly ground black pepper

Small fresh flat-leaf parsley sprigs, for garnish

¼ cup small olives, such as niçoise or Umbria, for garnish

Ease of Preparation: Moderate

To make the olive butter: Put the garlic, shallot, olives, and parsley in a food processor and pulse several times until the mixture is evenly chopped. Add the butter and mustard and pulse until the mixture is smooth. Season the butter with pepper and taste; if the flavors haven't quite come together, add a pinch or two of kosher salt and pulse again briefly.

Transfer the butter to a sheet of parchment or wax paper and shape into a log about 1¼ inches in diameter. Wrap tightly in the parchment and then again in plastic wrap and refrigerate for up to 5 days. To use, unwrap and slice into ¼-inch-thick coins. (Makes about ½ cup.)

To make the salmon: Heat an outdoor or stovetop grill to medium heat. Fill a medium saucepan half full with water, add a tablespoon of kosher salt, and bring to a boil. When the water boils, add the pasta, stir, and cook according to the package directions until just tender. Drain thoroughly (do not rinse), transfer to a warm bowl, and toss with 2 tablespoons of the olive butter. Cover the pasta with a tea towel to keep warm.

Meanwhile, season the salmon fillets with salt and pepper. Grill the fillets skin-side up for 8 minutes, rotating once to mark. Turn the salmon over and grill until just cooked through, about 2 to 3 minutes for a 1-inch fillet, longer if the fish is thicker. Just before removing the salmon from the grill, top each piece with a round of olive butter.

To serve, divide the pasta among 4 warm plates and set a salmon fillet on top, skin-side down. Top each piece of salmon with another thin round of olive butter, garnish with parsley and olives, and serve immediately with Roasted Golden Beets with Olives **(see recipe and pairing on next page)**.

Roasted Golden Beets with Olives

SERVES 4

The sweetness of the roasted beets is enhanced by quality olives. Be sure to start roasting the beets about an hour before you begin with the salmon.

1 pound beets, preferably golden, washed and trimmed of greens
2 tablespoons extra virgin olive oil
2 tablespoons taggiasca olives, or any oil-cured black olives, pitted
Grated zest of 1 lemon
1 tablespoon minced fresh flat-leaf parsley
Kosher salt
Freshly ground black pepper

Ease of Preparation: Easy

Preheat the oven to 350°F.

Put the beets in a shallow baking dish and drizzle with 1 teaspoon of the olive oil; toss to coat. Roast the beets until tender, about 45 minutes. Set the beets aside to cool slightly, then remove the skins with your fingers. (Wearing kitchen gloves will prevent the beets from staining your fingers.)

Cut the beets into wedges and transfer them to a serving bowl. Add the olives, lemon zest, parsley, and remaining olive oil; toss to combine. Season with salt and pepper and keep the beets warm until ready to serve.

> **PAIRING** Salmon and Pinot Noir are a classic match; the fruitiness and fuller body of a Russian River Valley Pinot will pair well with this dish, mirroring the richness and sweetness of the beets and matching the earthiness of the olives; recommended producers include Hartford Court, Rochioli and Merry Edwards.

Duck Breast with Caramelized Apples and Lavender Honey

SERVES 4

Duck is often served with orange or cranberry sauce, as the sweet-tart qualities of those fruits complement the rich meat so well. In this recipe from Tartine in Westport, Connecticut, tart apples and lavender honey perform the same function. The lavender honey transports the dish to the south of France. (But if you can't find it, any wild honey will do.)

4 Peking or Moulard duck breasts

Salt and freshly ground black pepper

¼ cup extra virgin olive oil

¼ cup lavender honey (or other wild honey)

2 tablespoons unsalted butter

1 teaspoon vegetable oil

8 Granny Smith or Fuji apples, peeled, cored, each cut into 8 sections

2 tablespoons sugar

2 pounds fresh spinach, stemmed, rinsed, and patted dry

¼ cup dried lavender flowers or fresh thyme leaves, for garnish

Ease of Preparation: Moderate

Pierce the skin on each duck breast lightly with a fork. Turn over and season the meat with salt and pepper.

Heat 2 tablespoons of the olive oil in a large ovenproof sauté pan over medium-high heat until it ripples. Place the duck breasts, skin-side down, in the pan and cook. Using a spatula or tongs, lift the breasts every minute or so to keep them from sticking. As the duck fat builds up in the pan, use a spoon to remove the fat and maintain the original oil level. Cook the duck until the skin starts to crisp and turn dark brown, about 15 minutes. Remove from the heat.

Preheat the oven to 400°F.

Turn the breasts over so that they are meat-side down. Brush the skin, now facing up, with about 1 tablespoon of the honey. Place the pan in the oven and roast for 7 minutes (for medium-rare). Remove the breasts from the pan, place on a cutting board, and let rest for 10 to 15 minutes.

Meanwhile, in another pan, heat the butter and vegetable oil over medium-high heat until the butter is melted. Add the apples and sugar and cook, stirring often, until they start to brown, or caramelize, about 10 minutes. Lower the heat and continue to cook until the slices soften, making sure the sugar does not burn.

In a third pan, heat the remaining 2 tablespoons olive oil over medium-high heat until it ripples. Slowly add the spinach and stir until it starts to wilt, 3 to 5 minutes. Season with salt and pepper to taste. Divide the spinach evenly among 4 dinner plates.

Thinly slice 1 duck breast, and place the slices on a dinner plate, fanning them out in a semicircle around the mound of spinach. Repeat with the remaining duck breasts. Divide the apple mixture evenly among the plates, arranging most on the opposite side of the spinach from the duck and a few on top of the spinach.

Drizzle the remaining honey over each serving and around the edge of each plate. Garnish with lavender flowers, if using, or thyme leaves. Serve immediately.

PAIRING The herbal, floral notes of this dish will be echoed by an aromatic red Burgundy; recommended communes include Hautes Côtes de Nuits, Nuits-Saint-Georges, Volnay, and Savigny-Les-Beaune.

Rice with Lamb Ribs

Uighur Autumn Pulao

SERVES 4 TO 6

This recipe is adapted from one found in Jeffrey Alford and Naomi Duguid's *Seductions of Rice*. A *pulao*, also known in other countries as *pilaf*, is a dish from India and Pakistan, where it is made with basmati rice. This variation comes from the Uighurs, a Turkic people who live in the Silk Road oases in Xinjiang, in western China. Here, the dish, which is often served for special occasions, is made with short-grain red rice, such as a Bhutanese red, and lamb back ribs. If you can't find lamb back ribs, use boneless shoulder chunks or shoulder chops instead.

3 cups short-grain red rice, such as Bhutanese red rice, rinsed, or medium- or short-grain rice

4 teaspoons salt

⅓ cup vegetable oil

¼ cup rendered lamb fat (see Note)

1½ pounds lamb back ribs, rinsed, trimmed of fat, and cut into 3-inch chunks (left on the bone)

1 large onion, sliced

3 large carrots, cut on the diagonal into ¼-inch-thick slices, then into matchsticks

1 medium tomato, coarsely chopped

2 teaspoons sugar

1 large quince, cored and cut into 6 or 8 wedges, or 2 Granny Smith apples, cored and quartered

1 large red bell pepper, seeded, membranes discarded, and cut into 8 chunks

Ease of Preparation: Moderate to Difficult

Place the rice in a medium bowl and cover with warm water. Stir in 2 teaspoons of the salt and let soak while you prepare the other ingredients.

In a large, heavy wok or heavy pot, heat the oil and lamb fat over high heat almost to smoking, then add 1 teaspoon of salt. Add the lamb and brown on all sides, about 10 minutes. Add the onion slices and cook for 5 minutes. Add the carrots and tomato and stir well. If they start to stick, lower the heat slightly and turn them with a spatula. Cook for about 8 minutes, then add the sugar. Cook for another 5 to 8 minutes, until the carrots are very limp and starting to turn golden brown. Skim off any excess fat floating in the pan.

Add 3 ½ cups water and the remaining 1 teaspoon salt. Boil over medium heat for 10 minutes. Taste and adjust the seasonings. Remove the meat and set aside. Drain the rice and add it to the pot. The water should just cover the rice; if necessary, add a little more water. Bring to a boil

and cook for 5 minutes. Place the quince and red pepper evenly over the top of the rice, then top with the lamb. Cover, reduce the heat to low, and let steam for 30 minutes. Remove from the heat and let rest for about 10 minutes. (If you can't hear it simmer, increase the heat just slightly without uncovering it.)

To serve, remove the meat, pepper, and quince and set aside. Mound the rice on a platter, then top with the meat, pepper, and quince. Traditionally, the host removes the chunks of meat and slices them at the table, then returns them to the platter.

NOTE: To render lamb fat, cut about ½ pound lamb fat into small chunks. Place in a heavy skillet over medium heat. Stir to prevent burning as the fat begins to melt. After about 20 minutes, all the fat will have melted, leaving only small crisp cracklings. Strain rendered fat through a paper towel-lined sieve. (Yields about ½ cup liquid fat.)

PAIRINGS The relative richness of this dish calls for a red wine with crisp acidity such an Italian Barbera; recommended producers include Vietti and Michele Chiarlo.

Lamb with Apricots

Sali Boti

SERVES 4

This recipe was adapted from one by Ashok Bajaj, owner of the Bombay Club in Washington, D.C. The combination is of Parsi, or Persian, origin and contains the mixture of fruit, meat, and spices that is common to Parsi-inspired Indian cooking. Garam masala is an Indian spice blend available in the spice section of many supermarkets.

GINGER-GARLIC PASTE

1 (1½-inch) piece fresh ginger, peeled and coarsely chopped

4 garlic cloves

2 tablespoons water

LAMB

¼ cup sugar

¼ cup red wine vinegar

4 to 6 dried pitted apricots

4 cups plus 2 tablespoons vegetable oil

1 medium russet potato, julienned

1 medium onion, finely chopped

1 tablespoon ginger-garlic paste (see above)

1 medium tomato, finely chopped

1 teaspoon turmeric

1 teaspoon garam masala

1 teaspoon chili powder (optional)

2 pounds lamb, cut into bite-sized cubes

1 cup plain yogurt, whipped until smooth

Salt and freshly ground black pepper

Ease of Preparation: Moderate to Difficult

To make the ginger-garlic paste: Combine the ginger, garlic, and water in a food processor fitted with the metal blade and process until smooth. Set aside. The paste can be kept, covered, in the refrigerator for up to 1 month.

To prepare the lamb: Heat the sugar in a small, heavy saucepan over high heat until golden brown. (Be careful not to let the sugar burn, or to touch the hot sugar, as it can cause serious burns.) Carefully add the vinegar and apricots and stir to combine. Remove the pan from the heat and set aside.

In a large, heavy saucepan set over medium-high heat, heat 4 cups of oil (or enough oil to cover the potatoes and allow them to move a bit in the pan) until it sizzles. (Use a pan that's big enough; the oil should not come more than halfway up the sides of the pan.) When a deep-frying thermometer registers 365°F, add the potatoes and fry until golden. Using a slotted spoon, transfer the potatoes to paper towels to drain. (If you do not have a deep-frying thermometer, test the hotness of the oil by dropping a small piece of bread into the oil. If it browns immediately, the oil is ready. The oil should not smoke; if it does, it is too hot.)

Heat the remaining 2 tablespoons oil in a large, heavy sauté pan set over high heat until it sizzles. Add the onion and cook, stirring, for 5 to 10 minutes, until light golden. Add 1 tablespoon of the ginger-garlic paste and cook, stirring, for 1 to 2 minutes. Add the chopped tomato and cook, stirring, for 1 to 2 minutes. Add the turmeric, garam masala, chili powder if using, and lamb. Cook, stirring, for about 5 minutes.

Add the yogurt and bring to a boil. Immediately reduce the heat to medium-low and cook for 30 to 40 minutes, or until the lamb is tender and cooked through.

Add the caramelized sugar and apricot mixture to the lamb and mix thoroughly. Season with salt and pepper to taste. Pour the lamb mixture into a serving bowl and top it with the golden fried potatoes. Serve immediately.

> **PAIRINGS** Match the warm spice of the lamb with wines of similar character, such as Oregon Pinot Noir from Domaine Drouhin or a lighter-weight Syrah, such as a Crozes-Hermitage, or a St.-Joseph from producer Philippe Faury.

Spicy Grilled Shrimp Stew

Caldo de Camarón Asado

SERVES 12 AS AN APPETIZER, OR 6 AS A MAIN COURSE

Adapted from *Bayless's Mexico: One Plate at a Time* by Mexican food authority, Chicago chef-restaurateur, and cookbook author Rick Bayless, this unusual stew of tomatoey broth with spicy shrimp skewers calls for ingredients that are easy to find but deliver lusty, authentic flavor.

---

1 small white onion, cut in ¼-inch slices

3 garlic cloves, peeled and coarsely chopped

1½ pounds (9 to 12 medium plum or 3 medium-large round) tomatoes, chopped

2 tablespoons extra virgin olive oil, plus additional for brushing

6 cups chicken stock

1 to 2 large sprigs fresh epazote, or a small handful of fresh cilantro or parsley

2 pounds (about 48) medium-large shrimp

¾ teaspoon salt

About 2 tablespoons pure ground ancho or guajillo chile powder

3 medium (about 1½ pounds) sweet potatoes (or the purple-skinned Mexican sweet potatoes called *camotes morados*), peeled and sliced ½-inch thick

Fresh herb sprigs, for garnish (optional)

SPECIAL EQUIPMENT: **12 (7-inch) wooden skewers, soaked in water for 30 minutes and drained**

Ease of Preparation: Difficult

For the flavored stew base: In a blender or food processor, combine the onion and garlic with the tomatoes. Process to a smooth purée.

In a medium (4- to 5-quart) Dutch oven or Mexican *cazuela*, heat the olive oil over medium-high heat. When it's hot enough to make a drop of the purée sizzle, add the tomato mixture all at once and stir continually until it darkens in color and cooks down to the consistency of tomato paste, 10 to 12 minutes. Stir in the stock and the epazote. Partially cover the pot and simmer over medium-low heat for about 30 minutes.

To prepare the shrimp: While the broth is simmering, peel the shrimp, leaving their final joint and tail intact. Devein the shrimp and thread them on the skewers (4 per skewer), being careful not to bunch them too tightly. Lay them out flat on a tray and sprinkle them on both sides with salt and the ground chile.

To finish the dish: Heat a gas grill to medium or light a charcoal fire and let it burn until the coals are covered with gray ash and medium-hot. Add salt, if desired, to the broth; keep warm, covered, over low heat. Generously brush or spray the sliced sweet potatoes with olive oil, sprinkle both sides of each piece with salt, and grill, turning occasionally, until soft, 10 to 15 minutes. Divide the potatoes evenly among the soup bowls.

Lightly brush or spray the shrimp skewers with olive oil and lay them on the grill. Cook the shrimp until just pink, 2 to 3 minutes per side.

To serve, ladle the steaming broth over the potatoes in each soup bowl. Lay one (or two) skewers in each bowl (they'll rise from the broth). Garnish each serving with an herb sprig, if desired, and serve.

> **PAIRING** The tomatoes and spice in this dish call for a wine with pronounced acidity, such as a Mencía from Bierzo, Spain; recommended producers include Descendientes de J. Palacios, Dominio de Tares, and Luna Beberide.

Corn and Chile Stew with Duck and Shredded Cabbage

Pozole de Pato

SERVES 4

This recipe was adapted from Chef Richard Sandoval's book *Modern Mexican Flavors*. The original calls for hominy (which is traditional), but for summer, Sandoval says that fresh corn, grilled right on the cob, makes a delightful substitution.

POZOLE

8 ears corn, shucked

3 tablespoons canola oil

½ cup chopped white onion

2 garlic cloves, chopped

2 dried guajillo chiles, stemmed and seeded

4 cups duck or chicken stock

1 bay leaf

1 tablespoon honey

SALAD

1 cup shredded green cabbage

¼ cup shredded red radish (about 4 radishes), plus additional radishes, sliced, for garnish (optional)

1 tablespoon chopped fresh cilantro

2 teaspoons fresh lemon juice

¼ teaspoon salt

⅛ teaspoon freshly ground black pepper

4 boneless duck breast halves, with skin

Chile powder, for garnish

Ease of Preparation: Moderate

To make the pozole: Grill the shucked corn on a preheated gas or charcoal grill, turning it a few times, until the kernels start to color. Remove the ears from the grill and allow them to cool. When cool enough to handle, scrape the kernels off the cobs with a knife and set aside. Discard the cobs.

In a large saucepan, heat 1 tablespoon of the oil. Add the onion and garlic and sauté over medium-high heat for about 4 minutes, or until softened. Add the chiles and sauté for 30 to 45 seconds, or until slightly darkened. Add 2 cups of the stock and simmer for about 5 minutes, or until the chiles are softened.

Pour the chile mixture into a blender and purée. Strain the purée through a medium-mesh sieve back into the saucepan, pressing on the solids with the back of a ladle or rubber spatula. Discard the solids in the sieve.

Add the corn to the saucepan along with the bay leaf and the remaining stock and keep warm.

To make the salad: In a large bowl, stir together the cabbage, shredded radish, cilantro, lemon juice, salt, and pepper. Set aside.

Heat a large skillet over medium-high heat. Add the duck breasts, skin-side down, and sear for about 5 minutes, until crisp. Turn and sauté for 5 to 10 minutes longer, until cooked through. Transfer the duck breasts to a cutting board and let rest for 10 minutes. Slice each breast diagonally across the grain into 3 thin slices.

Add the honey to the posole and season to taste with salt and pepper.

To serve, divide the posole among 4 shallow soup bowls. Spoon ¼ cup of the cabbage salad into the center of each. Then, in each bowl, arrange 3 pieces of duck breast angled upright around the cabbage. If desired, garnish with radish slices and sprinkle the rims of the bowls with chile powder. Serve.

Aglaia's Moussaka

SERVES 8 TO 10

This recipe is adapted from *New Greek Cuisine* by Jim Botsacos, chef-partner of Molyvos restaurant in New York City. For this version of the Greek classic, Botsacos began with a recipe from Aglaia Kremezi, the Greek cookbook author and cooking teacher, which he liked because it was lighter than the typical rendition. He further lightened it by adding Greek yogurt to the béchamel sauce. Botsacos suggests fully cooking all the components of the dish the day before you plan to bake and serve it. Or you can assemble the moussaka and chill it for up to two days before baking. *Ras el hanout*, a Moroccan spice blend, and Aleppo pepper can be found at some specialty foods stores and ordered online from The Spice House (www.thespicehouse.com).

Ease of Preparation: Difficult

To make the yogurt sauce: Attach the bay leaf to the onion half by piercing it with the 2 cloves. Set aside. Combine the milk and cream in a medium, heavy saucepan over medium heat. Cook, without stirring, for 5 minutes, or just until the mixture begins to simmer. Remove from the heat and set aside.

Heat the butter in another medium, heavy saucepan over medium heat. When melted and hot, add the flour and cook, stirring constantly, until the mixture is thick and smooth. Cook, stirring constantly, for 10 minutes. Remove from the heat, and whisking constantly to prevent lumps from forming, add the hot milk mixture in a slow, steady stream.

When well blended, return the mixture to medium heat. Add the onion half and bring to a simmer. Simmer for 10 minutes. Season with salt, pepper, and nutmeg to taste. Remove from the heat and set aside to cool. When cool, fold in the yogurt and set aside until ready to use. You will have 4 cups. Reserve any leftover for another use.

YOGURT SAUCE

1 bay leaf

½ medium onion, peeled

2 whole cloves

1 ½ cups whole milk

1 ½ cups heavy cream

1 ½ tablespoons unsalted butter

½ cup all-purpose flour

Coarse salt and freshly ground black pepper

Freshly grated nutmeg

½ cup Greek yogurt (see page 106)

MOUSSAKA

¼ cup dried currants

1 (28-ounce) can whole plum tomatoes

2 cups olive oil, plus more if needed

1 pound 90% lean ground beef

1 pound lean ground lamb

Coarse salt and freshly ground black pepper

1 teaspoon *ras el hanout*, or more to taste

1 teaspoon Aleppo pepper, or more to taste

1 teaspoons ground cinnamon, or more to taste

4 cups finely diced onion

6 garlic cloves

2 cups dry red wine, such as Agiorgitiko, Cabernet Sauvignon, or Sangiovese

1 pound russet potatoes, cut into 18 (¼-inch-thick) slices

2 medium yellow or red bell peppers, cored, seeded, and diced

2 pounds eggplant, cut into 18 (¼-inch-thick) slices

3 cups yogurt sauce (see above)

1 cup (about ¼ pound) freshly grated kefalotyri or Parmesan cheese

To make the moussaka: In a small bowl, pour hot water to cover over the currants and let soak for 30 minutes.

Meanwhile, drain the tomatoes, reserving the juice. Using your hands, crush the tomatoes. Measure out 2 ½ cups and combine them with the reserved tomato juice; set aside. (You will probably have about ½ cup tomatoes left over. Save for another recipe.)

Place a large skillet over medium heat. When very hot but not smoking, add 2 tablespoons of the olive oil, swirling to coat the pan. Add about a quarter each of the beef and lamb and cook, stirring to break up the meat, for 5 minutes, or until the meat has browned lightly. Season with a generous pinch of salt and pepper and then with ¼ teaspoon each of *ras el hanout* and Aleppo pepper and a pinch of cinnamon. Using a slotted spoon, transfer the mixture to a colander placed in a mixing bowl. Return the pan to medium heat and repeat three times to brown and season all the meat. Discard the oil.

Return the skillet to medium heat. Add ¼ cup of the remaining olive oil and, when hot, add the onion along with a pinch of salt. Cover and cook, stirring occasionally, for about 10 minutes, or until the onion is soft and translucent. Add the garlic, stirring to just combine, and cook for another minute. Add the wine and cook, stirring occasionally, for about 25 minutes, or until the pan is almost dry. Add the reserved tomatoes along with their juice, stirring to combine. Bring to a simmer. Add the reserved meat mixture, stirring to combine well. (Take care, as the pan will be quite full.) Taste, and if necessary, season with additional *ras el hanout*, Aleppo pepper, and cinnamon. Lower the heat, and cook at a bare simmer for 6 to 8 minutes.

Drain the currants and stir them into the meat mixture. Taste and season with salt and pepper, if necessary. Cook for another 30 minutes. Transfer the meat mixture to a mixing bowl set over an ice bath to cool. When cool, set aside.

Place a large sauté pan over medium heat. When hot, add ½ cup of the remaining olive oil, swirling to coat the pan. When very hot, add the potato slices, 6 at a time, frying, turning occasionally, for about 15 minutes, or until golden. Transfer to a double layer of paper towels to drain. Repeat the process with the remaining potatoes, adding more oil as needed. When all of the potatoes have been fried, drain off half of the oil in the pan.

Return the pan to medium heat. When hot, add ¼ cup of the remaining olive oil, swirling to coat the pan. When very hot, add the peppers and sauté for about 5 minutes, or until just wilted. Season with salt and pepper to taste and remove from the heat. Transfer to a plate to cool.

Preheat the oven to 500°F.

Combine ½ cup of the remaining olive oil with salt and pepper to taste in a small bowl. Using a pastry brush, lightly coat both sides of the eggplant slices with the seasoned oil. Then season the slices with additional salt and pepper to taste. Place half of the slices on a baking sheet. Do not crowd the pan. Place in the preheated oven and roast for 6 to 8 minutes, or until lightly charred. Turn and roast for another 8 minutes, or until both sides are equally charred. Transfer to a platter to cool and repeat with remaining half of eggplant slices.

If baking the moussaka immediately, lower the oven temperature to 350°F. Place the potato slices in one even layer over the bottom of a 13 x 8 x 2-inch deep rectangular baking dish. Place the eggplant slices, slightly overlapping, in one even layer over the potatoes. Repeat with an even layer of peppers. Spoon the meat mixture over the peppers, spreading it out with a spatula to make an even layer. Top with a thin layer of béchamel and sprinkle with the cheese. At this point, the moussaka may be covered with plastic wrap and refrigerated for up to 2 days before baking. Place the moussaka on a baking sheet in the preheated oven and bake for 25 minutes, or until bubbling around the edges. Remove the moussaka from the oven and let it stand for about 10 minutes before serving.

NOTE: Greek yogurt is thicker and creamier than regular yogurt; it's available at specialty foods markets and some supermarkets. To make your own, place 1 cup regular plain yogurt in a sieve lined with a double thickness of cheesecloth. Set the sieve over a bowl and allow yogurt to drain and thicken in the refrigerator for 12 hours.

PAIRING The luxurious richness of this Greek favorite is balanced by the freshness and structure of a Greek Agiorgitiko; recommended producers include Palivou, Skouras, and Gaia.

Roasted Asparagus with
Aceto Balsamico Tradizionale di Modena

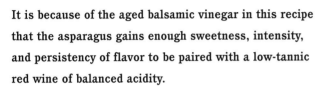

It is because of the aged balsamic vinegar in this recipe that the asparagus gains enough sweetness, intensity, and persistency of flavor to be paired with a low-tannic red wine of balanced acidity.

1 bunch (about 1 pound) thin-to-medium spears asparagus, trimmed

2 tablespoons extra virgin olive oil

Salt to taste

1 teaspoon *aceto balsamico tradizionale di Modena* (aged balsamic vinegar)

Ease of Preparation: Easy

Preheat the oven to 425°F.

Brush the asparagus lightly with the olive oil and arrange in a single layer on a broiler pan or baking sheet. Sprinkle with salt. Broil the asparagus 4 to 5 inches from the heat for 10 minutes, or until lightly browned, turning the spears after 5 minutes. Transfer the asparagus to a serving platter and drizzle with the balsamic vinegar. Serve at once.

NEVER SAY NEVER PAIRING

The sweetness, intensity, and persistent flavor of the aged balsamic in this dish pairs well with a low-tannin red with balanced acidity. Try it with a Tuscan Sangiovese; recommended regions include Chianti Classico, Morellino di Scansano, and Torgiano (Umbria).

About Fruit-Forward,
Medium-Bodied Red Wines

Probably the most versatile red wine in the world falls squarely in this category. Pinot Noir, which has its origins in France's Burgundy region but is now grown worldwide, is the quintessential medium-bodied, fruity red wine. Yes, some Pinots can be fairly well-oaked, which tends to mask some of the wine's inherent fruit character. And sometimes they can grow in size and weight if exposed to too much sunshine. But for the most part, Pinot Noir sits firmly on the equator between the wine world's big reds and its more streamlined ones.

The focus in wines labeled fruit-forward and medium-bodied—think of Pinot Noir as well as wines like Barbera, Sangiovese, Grenache, Cabernet Franc, Mencía, and several Greek varieties—is generally on the brightness and berry character of the wine more than power, oak, and tannin. Wines that fit this description flow across the palate and complement food more than taking over the palate and usurping the food's flavors.

Acidity is the key component in determining where a wine settles on the scale that starts at light-bodied and ends at full-bodied. And Sangiovese, the base grape for Chianti, Brunello, Vino Nobile and Morellino di Scansano, is renowned for its vibrant acids but also its depth of fruit, which makes it a first-round pick as far as medium-bodied, fruity wines go. Grenache from Châteauneuf-du-Pape and Côtes-du-Rhône brings some of Sangiovese's brightness but also a penchant for sweeter, riper and darker berry flavors. Meanwhile, Mencía, which hails from the Bierzo region of Spain, is another balanced, fruit-forward wine that does very well at the dinner table.

Geographically speaking, these wines frequently come from Mediterranean or quasi-Continental growing zones. To be sure, they do not do well in hot-climate regions, which is where the powerful reds are born and bred.

The best food pairings for fruit-forward, medium-bodied wines tend to be subtle. Mushrooms and truffles, rice dishes, duck, salmon, pork, and lamb are all good starting points if Pinot Noir, Chianti, or Côtes-du-Rhône is what you're drinking.

Chapter 5

Big, Powerful Red Wines

Big, powerful, red wines—these four words say it all. These reds are the special ones, the crème de la crème. Most often, these are the bottles that have been reserved for important occasions—anniversaries, birthdays, graduations, and holiday gatherings. These are the reds that are greatly anticipated. They are going to be savored. They are expected to be exceptional. The entrées with which they are paired are intentionally top-of-the-line, too.

In this chapter, fancy cuts of meat star. How could it be otherwise when you are serving a Châteauneuf-du-Pape? Not surprisingly then, you'll find recipes here for a rack of lamb (page 115), a tournedos of beef with a sauce of bleu d'Auvergne (page 122), a Brazilian *churrasco* of beef tenderloin (page 113). These are hardly everyday dinners, and the wines that accompany them are anything but *ordinaire*.

On a less formal note, you will also find a lovely, long-cooking recipe for lamb shanks with pomegranate and mint gremolata (page 118), which is suitable for any special occasion, and an amazing cassoulet (page 126)—a two-day project that is worth every ounce of the effort that goes into it.

One might wonder how a recipe for steak *frites* (steak with french fries, page 116) made its way into a chapter on big, powerful, red wines. The right cut of meat, of course, will justify the choice of wine. More interesting than that, though, is our Never Say Never selection: pasta with dandelion greens, chickpeas, ricotta salata, and a little (just a third of a cup) pancetta (page 128). No other meat. A nearly vegetarian recipe in a chapter on big red wines? That's right. A big red stands up to the pasta's medley of assertive flavors. It's all about power.

Churrasco

SERVES 4

Churrasco is Brazil's answer to barbecue, beloved by everyone from the *gauchos* (cowboys) working the nation's cattle ranches to their wealthy employers. Unlike the barbecue of the American South, the Brazilian version is typically flavored and tenderized with a simple mixture of water, salt, and garlic. Today, well-to-do families in Brazil's southern state of Rio Grande do Sul have open-fire pits in their homes. But don't call in the builders just yet—you can re-create a *churrasco* experience on your backyard grill.

Ease of Preparation: Easy

Mix the salt, garlic, and water together in a small bowl until the salt is dissolved.

Preheat a grill to medium-hot.

Skewer the meat lengthwise and place it on the preheated grill. Baste the meat throughout the slow-cooking process with the water mixture, turning the skewer regularly, until the meat reaches the desired degree of doneness—a meat thermometer inserted into the thickest part of the tenderloin will read about 115°F for rare, 120°F for medium rare or 130°F for medium. Serve with a variety of cold salads.

1 tablespoon kosher salt

1 garlic clove, mashed

1 cup warm water

1 (2-pound) beef tenderloin, preferably center cut

SPECIAL EQUIPMENT: **1 large metal skewer, long enough to skewer a whole tenderloin lengthwise**

PAIRING The robust flavors of an Argentinean Malbec are a natural with this South American classic; recommended producers include Catena Zapata, Bodega Norton, and Bodega Renacer/Punto Final.

Slow-Cooked Rack of Lamb

SERVES 2 TO 4

So traditional it's almost a cliché on restaurant menus, rack of lamb deserves its lofty status for one reason: it is delicious. But it's also very easy to prepare at home. Lowering the temperature and cooking it more slowly than is traditional results in juicy, succulent meat. If you prefer well-done meat, select a less expensive cut. Ask your butcher to french the rack of lamb for you, which means to cut the meat away from the end of the ribs or chops, making for a more attractive presentation.

1 rack of lamb, trimmed and frenched
Kosher salt
Freshly ground black pepper
1 cup dry red wine
1 fresh thyme sprig, plus additional sprigs, for garnish
1 small fresh rosemary sprig, plus additional sprigs, for garnish
1 cup meat stock (lamb, beef, or duck) or canned low-sodium beef broth
2 tablespoons butter, chilled

Ease of Preparation: Easy

Preheat the oven to 300°F.

Season the rack of lamb all over with salt and pepper. Set a small roasting rack over a heavy pan, set the lamb on the rack, and place on the middle rack of the oven. Cook for 30 to 40 minutes, until the temperature in the center of the middle rib reaches 125°F for rare, 130°F for medium-rare, or 140°F for medium. Transfer the roasting rack to a work surface and cover loosely with foil.

Set the roasting pan over high heat on top of the stove, add the wine and herbs, and cook, stirring to loosen any bits of meat, until the wine is reduced to about 3 tablespoons. Add the stock and cook until rich and thick. Taste the sauce and season with salt and pepper. Remove the sauce from the heat and discard the herb sprigs.

Warm dinner plates. Whisk 1 tablespoon butter into the sauce and when it is completely incorporated, whisk in the remaining butter. Taste and adjust the seasoning, if necessary. Cover the pan and set aside briefly. Carve the rack of lamb between the rib bones. Spoon pools of sauce in the center of each warm plate, set the lamb on top, garnish with herb sprigs, and serve immediately.

> **PAIRING** The structure and complexity of a Napa Valley Cabernet Sauvignon or Bordeaux complement the assertive flavors of this dish; recommended producers include Hartwell, Harlan, and Caymus in Napa, and Châteaux Sociando-Mallet, Léoville-Barton, and Vieux Château Certan in Bordeaux.

Steak Frites

SERVES 4

This traditional bistro recipe is from Josh Moulton, formerly executive chef at Bleu Café in Greenwich, Connecticut. Here the *frites*, or French fries, are cooked twice (the secret to getting really crisp fries). For delicious results, do the first round of frying a day ahead, chill the fries, and fry again just before serving. And, if you don't have a cooking thermometer, heat the oil, then test it by submerging one fry; if the fry pops up and floats, the oil is hot enough for cooking.

FRITES

8 russet potatoes, peeled and cut into ½-inch-thick sticks

Soybean oil (enough to fill the pan to a depth of 3 inches)

STEAKS

4 (10-ounce) sirloin steaks, each about 1½ inches thick

Sea salt

Freshly ground black pepper

SPECIAL EQUIPMENT: **deep-fat or candy thermometer**

Ease of Preparation: Moderate

To make the frites: Line a large baking pan with a double layer of paper towels.

In a large, deep pot, heat the oil over medium-high heat to 250°F on a deep-fat thermometer. Add the potatoes and blanch them until they are soft all the way through but not crisp or colored, 4 to 5 minutes. Using a slotted spoon, remove the potatoes from the oil to drain on the towel-lined pan. Reserve the oil for later use in the recipe. Remove the used towels, replace with fresh ones, and spread the potatoes out in a single layer, using more lined pans if necessary. Refrigerate for at least 1 hour or overnight, ideally 24 hours.

Before serving, preheat a charcoal or gas grill or the broiler. Season the steaks generously with salt and pepper. Grill or broil the steaks to the desired degree of doneness, 7 to 9 minutes for rare, 9 to 12 minutes for medium rare and 11 to 13 minutes for medium. Transfer the steaks to a serving platter and let stand, loosely covered, for 5 minutes.

While the steaks are resting, remove the potatoes from the refrigerator. Heat the reserved oil in a large, deep pot to 350°F. Add the blanched potatoes and deep-fry them until crisp and golden. Remove the potatoes with a slotted spoon to drain briefly on paper towels. Transfer the potatoes to a serving bowl and serve at once with the steaks.

PAIRING The ripe fruit of a Sonoma County Merlot or Zinfandel is the perfect counterpoint to these simply grilled steaks; recommended Merlot producers include Kendall-Jackson, Longboard, and Pride Mountain, and recommended producers for Zinfandel include Greenwood Ridge, DeLoach, and Rosenblum.

Vella's Pasta alla Campagna

Penne with Bacon, Swiss Chard, Dry Jack Cheese, and Pecans

SERVES 4 TO 6

Joann Snyder, a long-time Vella Cheese employee, created this exuberant recipe for the first edition of *A Cook's Tour of Sonoma.* It calls for dry Monterey Jack cheese, an aged cheese that originated in California. If you can get Golden Bear Dry Monterey Jack Cheese—aged for 2 to 4 years—this recipe is a great way to use it; its nuttiness and depth of flavor is perfect in this complex (but easy to make) dish.

1 pound bacon, diced

1 pound Swiss chard

1 tablespoon Dijon mustard

3 tablespoons red wine vinegar

1 tablespoon kosher salt

12 ounces penne

3 tablespoons olive oil

3 garlic cloves, pressed

½ teaspoon red pepper flakes

Freshly ground black pepper

8 ounces Golden Bear Dry Monterey Jack Cheese or other aged Dry Monterey Jack cheese, grated (2 cups)

1 cup pecans, coarsely chopped and toasted

Ease of Preparation: Moderate

Cook the bacon in a large saucepan or sauté pan set over medium heat until it is just crisp. Using a slotted spoon, transfer bacon to paper towels to drain. Discard all but 3 tablespoons of the bacon fat. Set the pan aside.

Wash the Swiss chard, dry it thoroughly, and remove the stems. Trim and discard the base of the stems, and cut the stems into thin slices. Cut the leaves crosswise into ½-inch-thick strips. Keep the leaves and stems separate and set both aside. In a small bowl, mix together the mustard and vinegar and set the mixture aside.

Bring a large pot of water to a boil, add the 1 tablespoon kosher salt, and cook the pasta according to the package directions until just tender. Drain thoroughly (do not rinse).

While the pasta cooks, add the olive oil to the reserved bacon fat in the pan and heat over medium-low heat; when hot, add the chard stems, garlic, and red pepper flakes and sauté until the chard stems are tender. Add the chard leaves, cover the pan, and cook until the leaves are wilted, about 4 or 5 minutes. Season with salt and pepper and remove from the heat.

Place the hot pasta in a large bowl, pour the mustard mixture over it, and toss thoroughly. Add the chard mixture, grated cheese, and three-quarters of the pecans and toss again. Top with the remaining pecans. Serve immediately.

> **PAIRING** The richness of the cheese and the smokiness of the bacon call for the similar flavors of Washington State Syrah; recommended producers include Cayuse, K Vintners, and Glen Fiona.

Lamb Shanks in Red Wine with Pomegranate and Mint Gremolata

SERVES 4

This recipe is adapted from a recipe in *The PlumpJack Cookbook* by Jeff Morgan. When it appeared in *Wine Enthusiast,* he noted, "This copious, rustic dish is topped with an elegant, fresh mint sauce. The mint is paired with a single tablespoon of intense pomegranate molasses, which can be found on the syrup shelf of many supermarkets. Ask your butcher to 'crack' the lamb shanks, which allows them to cook a little faster than they would otherwise. This recipe can be doubled or tripled." You can also look for pomegranate molasses at Middle Eastern markets and in the ethnic foods aisle of the supermarket. This recipe calls for kosher wine because it was created to be a Passover recipe, but you can use any wine you like.

SHANKS

4 lamb shanks, cracked

Salt and freshly ground black pepper

4 tablespoons extra virgin olive oil

1 onion, coarsely chopped

1 carrot, peeled and coarsely chopped

2 celery ribs, coarsely chopped

10 garlic cloves, coarsely chopped

2 bay leaves

2 fresh rosemary sprigs

4 to 5 cups dry kosher red wine

GREMOLATA

Extra virgin olive oil as needed, plus ½ cup

3 medium to large garlic cloves, peeled and left whole

1 tablespoon pomegranate molasses

10 to 12 sprigs fresh mint

4 fresh flat-leaf parsley sprigs

Ease of Preparation: Moderate

Preheat the oven to 375°F.

To make the lamb shanks: Trim the excess fat from the lamb shanks and sprinkle them with salt and pepper. In a Dutch oven or large, ovenproof pot, heat 2 tablespoons of the olive oil over high heat. Sear the lamb shanks on both sides, 2 to 3 minutes. Remove from the pot and set aside.

Lower the heat to medium and add the remaining 2 tablespoons oil. Add the onion, carrot, celery, garlic, bay leaves, and rosemary, and sauté, stirring occasionally, until the onion becomes translucent, about 10 minutes. Add 4 cups of the wine, stirring to break up any solids that may have stuck to the bottom of the pot. Raise the heat to high and return the shanks to the pot. Add more wine, if necessary, to cover most of the shanks with liquid. When the wine begins to boil, cover the pot, and place it in the oven. Cook until the lamb shanks are very tender, 2 to 2½ hours.

To make the gremolata: In a saucepan, pour enough olive oil over the garlic cloves to cover them completely. Heat the oil over medium heat until it begins to bubble. Reduce the heat to low and simmer for 30 minutes. Reserve the garlic. (You can save the garlic-infused oil for garnish or cooking; store in a covered container for up to 2 weeks.)

Place the garlic cloves with the pomegranate molasses, mint, parsley, and the remaining ½ cup oil in a blender and pulse to blend well. Reserve at room temperature until ready to use.

To serve, arrange a lamb shank on each plate and top it with a spoonful or two of the gremolata. Spoon the pan juices from the cooked lamb onto each plate as well. Serve immediately.

PAIRING An Australian Shiraz has the richness to stand up to this traditional braise. Many even have a hint of mint to match the gremolata; recommended producers include Glaetzer, Penfolds, and Cape Mentelle.

Roast Duckling with Merlot-Chocolate Sauce and Roasted Beets

SERVES 2 TO 4

Chef David Page, co-owner of Shinn Estate Vineyards, chef-owner of Home Restaurant in New York City, and creator of this recipe, simmers a whole duckling in water to render some of the fat before roasting it. He says that pricking the skin after 20 minutes of roasting keeps it tender and flavorful, while allowing excess fat to be rendered slowly.

PAIRING What's more natural with Long Island duck than food-friendly L.I. Merlot? Recommended producers include Bedell, Shinn Estate, and Pellegrini.

DUCK

1 cup dry red wine, preferably Merlot

1 (4- to 5-pound) Long Island (Peking) duckling, fat cavities trimmed

3 fresh thyme sprigs

2 fresh bay leaves

8 black peppercorns

Rind of 1 orange, removed with a vegetable peeler

Salt and freshly ground black pepper

SPECIAL EQUIPMENT: **cheesecloth and twine**

BEETS

6 medium beets, trimmed, cut in half or quartered

4 to 5 garlic cloves

2 fresh thyme sprigs

2 tablespoons olive oil

Salt and freshly ground black pepper

SAUCE

½ cup dry red wine, preferably Merlot

2½ cups duck stock, veal stock, or dark chicken stock

2 fresh thyme sprigs

Grated zest and juice of ½ orange

1 tablespoon grated bitter unsweetened chocolate (such as Scharffenberger or Valrhona)

Salt and freshly ground black pepper

Ease of Preparation: Moderate

Preheat the oven to 400°F.

To make the duck: Simmer the red wine in a saucepan over medium-high heat for 15 minutes, until reduced in volume by two-thirds. Cool and set aside.

Bring a large pot of water to a simmer over high heat. Submerge the whole duck in the water and simmer for 3 minutes. Remove and let cool completely. Pat the duck dry. Set the duck, breast skin-side up, on a wire rack set in a roasting pan.

Place the thyme, bay leaves, peppercorns, and orange rind on a square of cheesecloth, bring the corners up to form a bundle, and tie the sachet off with the twine. Season the inside and outside of the duck with salt and pepper. Insert the sachet into the cavity of the duck. Roast for 20 minutes, periodically spooning any rendered fat out of the pan. Reserve the fat for another use.

While the duck is roasting, prepare the beets: Place the beets, garlic, thyme, and olive oil on a foil-lined baking sheet. Season with salt and pepper. Place in the oven with the duck.

At this point, prick the skin in the fatty parts of the duck, just below the breast and under the thigh. Reduce the oven temperature to 325°F and continue to roast the duck and beets for another 1½ hours, periodically spooning the rendered fat out of the pan.

After 1½ hours, use a pastry brush to baste the entire duck with the reduced red wine.

Raise the oven temperature to 400°F and roast the duck for 10 to 15 minutes more, until the bird is glazed. Remove the duck and beets from the oven and let the duck rest for 15 minutes before removing the sachet. Transfer the duck to a carving board, carve, and arrange the pieces on a serving platter along with the beets.

To make the sauce: Heat the wine in a small saucepan over medium-high heat for 7 minutes, or until reduced in volume by two-thirds. Add the stock, thyme, and orange zest and juice and reduce again by two-thirds. Just before serving, remove the pan from the heat, add the grated chocolate, one teaspoon at a time, whisking until it is incorporated. Season the sauce with salt and pepper. Strain through a fine-mesh strainer into a sauceboat and serve alongside the duck.

Tournedos au Bleu with Potatoes au Gratin and Sautéed Green Beans

SERVES 4

French Chef Eric Masson, former chef-owner of the Saratoga Lake Inn in Saratoga Springs, New York, prefers to use bleu d'Auvergne, a mild cow's milk blue cheese from the Auvergne region of France, for the sauce for these special cuts of beef. Masson notes that not every blue can be made into a sauce; this specific one melts evenly and lends a robust but not overpowering flavor.

PAIRING The smoky, herbal complexity, and prominent acidity of an Old World Syrah will help cut the richness of this Old World dish; recommended wines include Paul Jaboulet Aîné's Crozes-Hermitage, M. Chapoutier's and E. Guigal's Hermitage, and Tenuta Rapitala from Sicily. A more decadent match pairs a powerful Châteauneuf-du-Pape, like Domaine du Pegaü, with the dish's rich flavors.

POTATOES

4 russet potatoes, peeled and sliced ⅛ inch thick

¼ cup milk

¼ cup heavy cream

Pinch of salt

Pinch of freshly ground black pepper

Pinch of freshly grated nutmeg

1 cup shredded Swiss cheese

BEEF

4 (8-ounce) tournedos of center-cut beef tenderloin

Salt and freshly ground black pepper

GREEN BEANS

2 tablespoons olive oil

2 garlic cloves, minced

½ pound haricots verts (green beans)

SAUCE

½ cup heavy cream

¼ pound bleu d'Auvergne, Roquefort, or other blue cheese, cut into cubes

Ease of Preparation: Moderate

Preheat the oven to 375°F.

To make the potatoes: Layer the sliced potatoes in a shallow 9-inch square baking dish. Pour the milk and cream over them and sprinkle with salt, pepper, and nutmeg. Sprinkle the cheese evenly over the surface. Bake for 45 minutes, or until the cheese bubbles and is golden. Remove from the oven and keep warm until ready to serve.

To cook the beef: Preheat the broiler or a gas grill to high. Season each tournedo with salt and pepper and place on a broiler pan or directly on the grill rack. Grill or broil 4 to 5 inches from the heat for 5 to 6 minutes per side for medium, or until desired doneness. Transfer the beef to a platter and let rest, loosely covered, for 5 to 8 minutes.

While the meat is resting, prepare the green beans: Heat the oil in a medium sauté pan over medium-high heat until it ripples. Add the garlic and cook, shaking the pan, for about 30 seconds, until slightly softened. Add the beans and toss until coated with the oil. Cook, stirring and shaking the pan, for 3 to 4 minutes, or until the beans are tender and crisp. Remove from the heat and keep warm until ready to serve.

To make the sauce: In a small saucepan, bring the cream to a simmer, being careful not to let it scorch. Add the blue cheese and whisk until melted and thoroughly combined. Remove from the heat and keep warm.

To serve, divide the beans and potatoes evenly among 4 dinner plates. Add a tournedo to each plate, then spoon a generous amount of the sauce over the beef. Serve immediately, with any sauce remaining in a sauceboat to serve at the table.

Baked Rigatoni with Eggplant and Sausage

SERVES 6 TO 8

This recipe adapts well: You can choose hot or sweet fennel-flavored sausage, mellow black olives or tart green ones, fresh mozzarella or the ordinary supermarket kind. When you're ready to bake, the secret to crisping the top without drying out the filling is a very hot oven.

1 pound hot or sweet Italian sausage links

1 medium eggplant, halved lengthwise and cut into ½-inch rounds

¼ cup plus 2 tablespoons extra virgin olive oil

Kosher or sea salt

2 small garlic cloves, lightly crushed

1 (35-ounce) can whole plum tomatoes in their juices

½ cup flavorful pitted black or green olives, slivered

Freshly ground black pepper

1 pound rigatoni

1½ cups coarsely grated mozzarella

1 cup grated Pecorino Romano cheese

½ cup fresh bread crumbs

Ease of Preparation: Moderate to Difficult

Preheat the oven to 400°F.

Put the sausages on a rimmed baking sheet or broiler pan and bake, turning them, until browned all over and cooked through, about 10 minutes. Cool on paper towels, then cut on the diagonal into ½-inch slices.

Blot the eggplant rounds with paper towels. Heat the ¼ cup olive oil over medium heat in a skillet large enough to hold all the eggplant in a single layer (or divide the eggplant slices and olive oil between two large skillets). Fry the slices, turning once, until browned and tender. Transfer to paper towels and sprinkle lightly with salt.

Heat the remaining 2 tablespoons olive oil in a large saucepan over medium-low heat. Cook the garlic until golden; remove the garlic from pan and discard. Add the tomatoes and their juices to the saucepan, crushing the tomatoes with your fingers. Stir in ½ teaspoon salt. Simmer briskly until fairly thick, about 10 minutes. Add the olives and black pepper to taste.

Meanwhile, bring 6 quarts cold water and 2 tablespoons salt to a boil in a large pot. Add the rigatoni, stir well, and cook until al dente. Drain the pasta and return to the pot; mix in the tomato sauce.

To assemble: Spoon half of the sauced pasta into an oiled 12 x 8-inch baking dish. Arrange the sausage and eggplant slices on top. Sprinkle with the mozzarella and half of the Pecorino Romano. Spoon the remaining pasta on top. Combine the remaining Pecorino with the bread crumbs and sprinkle evenly over the top. Cover the dish with aluminum foil. (At this point, the dish can be held an hour or two at room temperature or refrigerated for up to 12 hours. If refrigerated, bring to room temperature before baking.)

To bake: Preheat the oven to 425°F. Bake the pasta, covered, until heated through, about 15 minutes. Remove the foil and bake until the topping is lightly browned, about 5 minutes.

PAIRING Reds from Southern Italy are naturals with the flavors of eggplant, olive, and tomato. Primitivo from Salento works well, as does Aglianico from Campania; recommended producers include Mastroberardino, Feudi di San Gregorio, and Villa Matilde.

Cassoulet des Pyrénées

SERVES 6 TO 8

Making a cassoulet, the renowned dish of white beans, duck confit, and sausages from southwestern France, is a culinary undertaking. You'll need to start cooking early the day before your feast—and you must allow several hours of cooking time on the feast day itself. This spicy variation makes a luscious fall or winter stew that is best served straight from the casserole in which it is baked.

2 confit of Muscovy or Peking duck legs (see Note)

4 pounds dried cannellini beans, soaked overnight in water and drained

2 tablespoons extra virgin olive oil

2 pounds Spanish onions, diced

4 vine-ripened tomatoes, diced

2 quarts unsalted chicken stock or canned low-sodium chicken broth

2 pounds pancetta, cut into 1-inch cubes

5 garlic cloves

6 carrots, cut into 1 ¼-inch rounds

6 celery hearts, diced

Freshly ground black pepper

2 pounds Spanish chorizo sausage, cut into 1-inch rounds

1 ounce whole morel mushrooms

1 ¼ cups finely chopped fresh flat-leaf parsley

1 cup plain bread crumbs

Ease of Preparation: Difficult

The day before your cassoulet feast, remove the duck confit from the refrigerator and let it come to room temperature so that the fat separates easily from the meat.

Meanwhile, place the cannellini beans in a large bowl and pour in enough boiling water to cover. Let the beans soak for at least an hour, or until they have absorbed the bulk of the water and doubled in size. Drain the beans and discard the soaking water. Set aside.

Using a wooden spoon, separate the softened confit duck legs from the fat that surrounds them and spoon the fat into a 4-quart Dutch oven, reserving 2 to 3 tablespoons of the fat for later. Cover and return the duck legs and reserved duck fat to the refrigerator. Set the Dutch oven over medium heat, add the olive oil and Spanish onions and sauté, shaking the pan and stirring, for 4 to 5 minutes, or until the onions are soft and translucent. Add the tomatoes and cook, stirring occasionally, until softened.

Pour in the stock. Add the pancetta, garlic, carrots, celery, and pepper to taste. Bring to a boil, reduce the heat to low, and cook for 90 minutes, or until the vegetables are softened, making a ragout. Add the drained beans. Simmer for 3 to 4 hours. Remove from the heat and let cool. Skim the fat from the surface, cover, and refrigerate overnight.

The following day, remove the vegetable ragout and duck confit from the refrigerator and let stand for 1 hour.

Place the duck confit in the top of a double boiler set over simmering water and heat for 5 minutes. Cool for 10 minutes. Pull the meat off the bones and cut into chunks and strips.

Preheat the oven to 375°F.

Grease a 4-quart casserole that can double as a serving dish with the reserved duck fat or olive oil. Transfer the ragout to the prepared dish. Add the duck meat, chorizo, and morels. Stir to distribute the ingredients. Cover the casserole with its lid or foil and bake for 1 hour.

Remove the cassoulet from the oven and remove the foil cover. Skim any excess fat from the surface. Stir in the parsley. Sprinkle the bread crumbs over the surface. Reduce the oven temperature to 325°F and return the cassoulet to the oven; bake for 1½ hours. A crust will form on top.

Remove the cassoulet from the oven and let stand for 10 minutes. Spoon cassoulet into dinner bowls and serve.

NOTE: To purchase duck leg confit (duck legs fully cooked and sealed in their own fat), contact d'Artagnan, the reputable purveyor of game and other specialty food products, online at www.dartagnan.com or by telephone at (800) 327-8246.

PAIRING The tannic rusticity of a Madiran or Cahors matches the heartiness of this regional specialty; recommended producers include Château d'Aydie in Madiran and Château Lagrezette in Cahors.

Orecchiette with Dandelion Greens and Chickpeas

SERVES 6 TO 8 AS A FIRST COURSE OR 4 AS A MAIN COURSE

This rustic dish captures the southern Italian delight in balancing assertive flavors: the bitterness of dandelion greens, heat of crushed red pepper, sharpness of ricotta salata, and subtle sweetness of currants. Serve as a first course if you like, but bear in mind that it's nutritionally well-balanced enough to make a great one-dish meal.

2 to 3 whole canned plum tomatoes with their juice (about 1 cup)

1 (14-ounce) can chickpeas, drained and rinsed

¼ cup extra virgin olive oil

1 small onion, sliced

4 slices pancetta, cut into ¼-inch pieces (about ⅓ cup)

Kosher or sea salt

1 bunch dandelion greens, stemmed, or broccoli rabe

1 pound orecchiette

Crushed red pepper flakes

2 cups crumbled ricotta salata cheese

2 tablespoons dried currants

¼ cup pine nuts or almonds, toasted

Ease of Preparation: Moderate

Combine the tomatoes and half of the chickpeas in a food processor with 1 cup water; process until smooth.

Heat the oil in a large skillet over medium heat. Sauté the onion and pancetta, stirring often, until lightly browned. Add the rest of the chickpeas and cook a minute or two longer. Stir in the puréed chickpea mixture. Reduce the heat until the mixture is barely simmering.

Meanwhile, combine 6 quarts water with 2 tablespoons salt in a large pan. Bring to a boil. Cook the dandelion greens or broccoli rabe a minute or two just until limp; remove with tongs and cool under running water. Add the pasta to the boiling water, stirring well. While the pasta cooks, coarsely chop the greens (makes about 2 packed cups). Stir the greens into the chickpea sauce. Add salt and crushed red pepper to taste.

When the orecchiette is al dente, reserve about a cup of the cooking liquid, then drain. Return the pasta to the pan and mix in the sauce, adding pasta water as needed for a saucy consistency. Stir in half of the ricotta salata and all of the currants. Spoon the pasta into shallow soup bowls, and sprinkle the remaining ricotta salata and the pine nuts on top. Serve immediately.

> **NEVER SAY NEVER PAIRING**
> The big, fruity profile of a Negroamaro or Primitivo from southern Italy is needed to temper the bitterness and spice of this pasta dish; recommended producers include Tormaresca, Taurino, and Vigne & Vini.

About Big, Powerful Red Wines

The heavyweights of the wine world, the meat-and-potatoes wines, the wines that attract collectors and fetch high prices—these are your powerful, full-bodied reds. And where do most people look when they are thirsty for something giant, something tannic, and something rippled with deep berry, cassis, and chocolate flavors? To Napa Valley, Washington State, Australia, and the Bordeaux region of France.

Cabernet Sauvignon ranks as the granddaddy among powerful reds, and nowhere is this wine made bigger and richer than in America's very own Napa Valley, which began to garner attention in the 1960s and 1970s and has only continued to grow in reputation since then. Today, Napa Cabernet—with its sheer, pure heft—is the poster child for big, powerful wines that are meant to be matched with grilled red meat, potent cheeses, and much more. Other areas of the world known for producing very good and sometimes world-class Cabernet Sauvignon include Washington's Columbia Valley and Chile's Maipo Valley.

Bordeaux, with its vaunted classified-growth blends of Cabernet Sauvignon, Merlot, and Cabernet Franc, has more history going for it than any other wine-producing region in the world. In warmer years, Bordeaux reds from communes such as Pauillac, Saint-Julién, and Pomerol can be huge, fleshy, and approachable. In other years, the wines are more subtle, tannic, and balanced, while in cool and wet years the wines can be downright underripe and vegetal. Consistency may not be Bordeaux's calling card, but that only adds to the appeal when the wines are great.

For more consistently sun-drenched reds that always have a combination of richness and power, many wine lovers have been turning to Australia for its Shiraz (aka Syrah) and Argentina for its Malbec. Because both countries have abundant sunshine and not much summer rain, ripeness is almost never an issue. However, if there's a fault that critics often cite with respect to big reds from Australia and Argentina, it is that the wines are too soft and sunbaked, and thus lack structure and aging ability.

The Spanish Tempranillo can also make powerful reds, especially the modern-styled wines from Rioja and Ribera del Duero. If harvested ripe and late in the season, Tempranillo can show similarities to Cabernet, blending bold fruit with ample structure. Northern Italy's Nebbiolo-based Barolo and Barbaresco often require years of bottle aging to tame tough-as-stone tannins, but remain a formidable Old World dynamic duo. And back in the United States, there's always Zinfandel, which can reach natural alcohol levels of 16 percent without much effort.

When popping the cork on a fine Bordeaux, Napa Cab, Washington Syrah, Sonoma Zinfandel, Aussie Shiraz or Argentine Malbec, make Dr. Atkins smile in his grave by braising some short ribs or throwing a porterhouse on the grill. You won't be sorry.

Chapter 6

Champagne &
Sparkling Wines

The singular sound of a bottle of Champagne being opened—that wonderful pop!—means only one thing. Something special is about to happen: a toast, a party, a celebration of some kind. So it will come as no surprise that the recipes we've paired with Champagne—French Champagne, that is—are celebratory, too. With only one notable exception, all are elegant hors d'oeuvres, just the type of tidbit to go hand in hand with a flute of notable bubbly. They are out of the ordinary in other ways, too, offering unexpected flavor combinations in addition to luxe ingredients: baby lamb chops; phyllo pastry cups with a savory-sweet filling of raspberry jam and Brie; sautéed-in-butter smoked salmon-and-cheese croque monsieurs (with a touch of caviar for good measure); chicken liver pâté (made with Port) that does not take days to make. They will elevate your party to a gala affair—or at least a fabulous feast.

If, on the other hand, you are looking to pair Champagne with a main course, which is a departure and a unique pairing challenge, we have just the dish for you: pan-seared duck breast with spaetzle, chanterelles, and spinach purée. It, too, is celebratory, easier to pull off than it might at first appear, and just the entrée to make for a New Year's Eve *diner à quatre*.

The dishes we've paired with other sparkling wines may also surprise; they include three very different salads, a velvety corn soup with caviar and crème fraîche, a colorful frittata of assorted vegetables and chorizo, and a frozen soup composed of a sensational Champagne-and-elderflower sorbet and white peaches. Yes, sorbet made with Champagne, but served with a sparkling wine. How's that for the best of both worlds?

Marinated Baby Lamb Chops with Mango Chutney

MAKES 24 HORS D'OEUVRES

When properly frenched (trimming the meat away from the end of the chop, which your butcher can do for you), rib chops can be served as finger food. This recipe comes from Chef Daniel Escarament.

½ cup balsamic vinegar

⅓ cup olive oil

1 tablespoon fresh lemon juice

2 garlic cloves, crushed

Salt and freshly ground black pepper

24 small baby lamb rib chops, frenched

Fresh rosemary sprigs, for garnish

Mango chutney, for serving

Ease of Preparation: Easy

In a large nonreactive bowl, combine the balsamic vinegar, olive oil, lemon juice, garlic, and salt and pepper. Add the lamb chops, turning to coat them with the marinade. Cover and refrigerate the lamb for at least 2 hours, turning at least once. Drain the lamb and discard the marinade just before cooking.

Heat a large skillet over medium-high heat until hot. Add the lamb chops, in batches, and pan-sear until nicely browned on the outside but still pink within, about 4 to 5 minutes per side. Arrange the chops on a serving platter and cover loosely to keep warm.

To serve, garnish the platter with rosemary sprigs and serve with bowls of mango chutney.

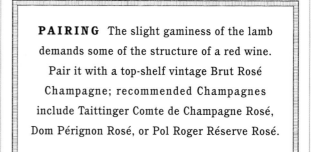

PAIRING The slight gaminess of the lamb demands some of the structure of a red wine. Pair it with a top-shelf vintage Brut Rosé Champagne; recommended Champagnes include Taittinger Comte de Champagne Rosé, Dom Pérignon Rosé, or Pol Roger Réserve Rosé.

Smoked Salmon and Caviar Croque Monsieur

SERVES 12

In an article entitled "The Ultimate New Year's Eve," which appeared in *Wine Enthusiast* in 2000, food writer Florence Fabricant shared her menu for the perfect New Year's Eve dinner. Luxurious is an understatement for the array of courses that included oysters, borscht, mushroom and foie gras pirozhkis, and these elegant French-style sautéed sandwiches, the recipe for which was adapted from Eric Ripert, chef at Le Bernardin, in New York City.

24 thin slices of fine-textured white bread, crusts removed

9 ounces Gruyère cheese, sliced paper-thin

10 to 12 ounces osetra or sevruga caviar, or best-quality American sturgeon caviar

12 slices smoked Atlantic salmon (about ½ pound)

¾ cup (12 tablespoons) clarified butter (see Note)

PAIRING The elegance of caviar and salmon calls for a classically structured vintage or nonvintage Brut Blanc de Blancs Champagne; recommended producers include Deutz, Lanson, and De Saint Gall.

Ease of Preparation: Moderate

Place the bread on a work surface. Cover 12 slices with a single layer of cheese. Spread a thin layer of caviar on the cheese. Cover each with one slice of the salmon, trimmed to fit exactly to the edge of the bread. Top each sandwich with the remaining slices of bread.

Heat 2 tablespoons of the clarified butter in a large nonstick skillet set over medium heat. Place several sandwiches in the skillet in a single layer and sauté, pressing down very gently with a spatula (but not forcing any of the caviar to ooze out) until lightly browned on one side. Add a little more butter, turn the sandwiches, and brown the second side. Remove the sandwiches to a warm platter and repeat until all sandwiches are fried.

To serve, cut each sandwich in half on the diagonal, arrange on a serving platter, and serve while still warm.

NOTE: To clarify butter, slowly melt 2 sticks cut-up unsalted butter in a heavy saucepan over low heat. As the butter melts, the milk solids will sink to the bottom, with a layer of clear butter on top. Carefully pour the clear—clarified—butter into a bowl, discarding the milk solids in the pan. Clarified butter is preferred here because when used for sautéing it burns less rapidly than butter with the milk solids intact.

Raspberry Phyllo Cups with Brie

MAKES 18

Elizabeth Parri Butler, president of Perfect Parties, a café and catering company based in Madison, Connecticut, says she likes this holiday finger-food recipe because the phyllo cups can be filled ahead of time and stored in the freezer for up to two weeks. At serving time, a quick turn in the oven is all they need.

4 sheets frozen phyllo dough, thawed

½ cup (1 stick) unsalted butter, melted

About 1 tablespoon raspberry preserves

½ pound Brie, rind removed, cut into 1-inch squares (⅛-inch thick)

36 fresh raspberries, for serving

Ease of Preparation: Easy to Moderate

To make the phyllo cups: Place 1 sheet of the phyllo on a work surface and brush with some of the melted butter. Top with another phyllo sheet and brush with melted butter. Repeat with the remaining 2 phyllo sheets. Using a 3-inch round metal cookie cutter (or other cylinder), cut the layered phyllo into 18 circles. If the dough sticks, run a sharp knife around the cutter.

Lightly butter 2 mini-muffin tins. Place 1 phyllo circle in the bottom of each of the 18 of the muffin cups and press gently with your fingertips to fit snugly. (One tin will be half filled.)

Preheat the oven to 350°F.

Bake the phyllo cups for 15 to 20 minutes, or until the phyllo is browned and has a nutty aroma. Leaving the phyllo cups in the muffin tins, place a tiny dollop of raspberry preserves (just a dot) into each. Top each with square of Brie. (At this point, the filled cups can be covered and frozen for up to 2 weeks. Before continuing, thaw them in the refrigerator for 6 hours.)

Place 2 fresh raspberries in each muffin cup and bake for 10 minutes, or until the Brie is melted and bubbly. Arrange the appetizers on a platter and serve immediately.

> **PAIRING** The sweetness of the raspberry here calls for the slight sweetness of a nonvintage demi-sec Champagne; recommended producers include Veuve Clicquot, Laurent-Perrier, and Heidsieck & Co. Monopole. Or just match the color by serving a sparkling rose.

Chicken Liver Pâté

SERVES 6

Laurent Tourondel, the executive chef and driving force behind the BLT group of restaurants in New York City, says he loves cooking with Port. For his recipe for a warm paté of chicken livers spread atop toasted country bread, Tourondel explains: "The addition of the Port adds sweetness and balance. The key to cooking with it, however, is not to reduce it on too high heat because it can get scorched and ruin the flavor."

PORT REDUCTION

1 bay leaf

2 fresh thyme sprigs

1 cup ruby Port

1 shallot, thinly sliced

1 garlic clove, thinly sliced

CHICKEN LIVERS

1 pound chicken livers, trimmed

1 tablespoon sea salt, plus additional to taste

¼ teaspoon pink salt (optional)

Freshly ground black pepper

2 tablespoons duck fat or extra virgin olive oil

2 tablespoons chopped shallot

2 tablespoons chopped garlic

3 tablespoons brandy or cognac

2 tablespoons unsalted butter, softened

5 fresh thyme sprigs

Fleur de sel

2 teaspoons extra virgin olive oil

6 thick slices country bread, toasted, for serving

Cornichons, for serving

Ease of Preparation: Moderate

To make the Port reduction: Tie the bay leaf and 2 thyme sprigs together with kitchen twine. In a small, heavy saucepan, bring the Port, herb bundle, shallot, and garlic to a simmer over medium-low heat. Cook until the Port is reduced to the consistency of thick syrup. Remove the herb bundle. Remove the pan from the heat and keep warm.

To make the chicken livers: Season half of the chicken livers with ½ tablespoon of the sea salt, some pink salt, if using, and pepper. Heat 1 tablespoon of the duck fat in a large skillet over high heat. When it ripples, add the seasoned livers and brown on one side, about 2 minutes. Turn and cook on the other side until golden brown but still pink in the center, about 1 minute more. Stir in 1 tablespoon each of the chopped shallot and garlic, then pour in 1 ½ tablespoons of the brandy and heat, about 2 minutes. Remove to a bowl and repeat with the remaining livers.

In a food processor fitted with the metal blade, combine the browned livers and Port syrup and process until smooth. Blend in the butter, and season to taste with additional sea salt and pepper. Scrape the mixture into a terrine or serving bowl.

To serve, remove the leaves from the remaining fresh thyme sprigs. Sprinkle the chicken liver pâté with the thyme leaves and fleur de sel and drizzle with olive oil. Serve warm with toasted country bread and cornichons.

PAIRING Pair this with a Port, of course, or try the opulence of a nonvintage Brut Rosé Champagne, which counters the rusticity of this peasant-style pâté; recommended producers include Veuve Clicquot, Canella, Piper-Heidsieck, and Billecart-Salmon.

Summer Melon Salad with Prosciutto

SERVES 6

The alcohol in this salad adds a delightful splash of flavor that works beautifully with both the sweet fruit and salty meat. Both the whiskey and the salt draw out the natural juices of the melon, making additional dressing unnecessary.

3 small melons (a mix of cantaloupe, Crenshaw, casaba, Charentais, honeydew, orange honeydew or green honeydew; do not use watermelon)

3 tablespoons whiskey, preferably Scotch

Freshly ground black pepper

Kosher salt

6 ounces prosciutto, very thinly sliced

1 head butter lettuce, leaves separated

1 cup raspberries

Ease of Preparation: Easy

Cut the melons in half and scoop out and discard the seeds. Peel one half of each melon and cut into ⅓-inch-thick wedges. Set the wedges in a wide shallow bowl.

Use a melon baller to cut balls from the reserved melon halves and add them to the bowl with the wedges. Sprinkle with the whiskey, add several turns of black pepper and two or three pinches of salt; cover and refrigerate for 30 to 60 minutes. Chill 6 dinner plates.

Cut half the prosciutto into ½-inch-wide crosswise slices. Set aside.

Put the butter lettuce into a large bowl, add several pinches of salt, and toss gently.

Place some of the chilled melon wedges on each plate, arranging them like the spokes on a wheel. Divide the lettuce among the plates, setting it in the center of each. Divide the whole slices of prosciutto among the servings, draping it across the melon wedges. Add the short strips of prosciutto and the raspberries to the melon balls, toss gently, and spoon some into the center of each plate, on top of the lettuce. Drizzle each serving with some of the juices in the bowl. Grind black pepper over each portion and serve immediately.

PAIRING The light and fruity character of Prosecco is a natural match for this sweet salad; recommended producers include Bisol, Astoria, and Mionetto.

Duck Breast with Spaetzle, Chanterelles, and Spinach Purée

SERVES 4

This recipe is from Brian Bistrong, formerly the executive chef of The Harrison restaurant in New York City. While the preparation looks elaborate, both the spaetzle and the spinach purée can be prepared one day in advance, leaving only the mushrooms and the duck breasts to be sautéed at the last minute.

SPAETZLE

1 cup all-purpose flour

1 egg

1 tablespoon crème fraîche

Milk, to thin the batter

Salt and freshly ground black pepper

1 tablespoon chopped fresh herbs, such as chives, parsley, and chervil

SPINACH PURÉE

1 tablespoon unsalted butter

1 shallot, minced

1 garlic clove, minced

1 pound fresh spinach, cleaned

2 tablespoons chicken stock, canned low-sodium chicken broth, or water

DUCK

4 boned Long Island (Peking) duck breasts, skin on

Salt and freshly ground black pepper

MUSHROOMS

2 tablespoons canola oil

½ pound chanterelle mushrooms, cleaned and sliced

Ease of Preparation: Moderate to Difficult

To make the spaetzle: Bring a large pot of water to a boil and fill a large bowl with water and ice. Meanwhile, in a medium bowl, combine the flour, egg, and crème fraîche. Drizzle in enough milk to form a thick batter. Season with salt and pepper and fold in the fresh herbs. Using a spaetzle maker or stainless steel colander, push the dough through the holes directly into the boiling water. When the spaetzle rise to the surface they are done. Scoop them up with a slotted spoon, and plunge into ice water to cool. Strain and toss with a little oil to keep from sticking. These can be made up to 1 day in advance and refrigerated in a covered container.

To make the spinach purée: Fill a large bowl with water and ice. Melt the butter in a large, heavy skillet over medium heat. Let the butter bubble until the white milk solids sink to the bottom and turn nut brown, about 4 minutes. Add the shallot and garlic and cook until soft and the shallot is translucent, about 8 minutes. Add the spinach and sauté until wilted. Season the spinach with salt and pepper and add the stock.

Transfer the spinach mixture to a blender or food processor and blend until smooth, then transfer to a metal mixing bowl. Place the bowl in the ice water and stir to cool the purée quickly (this will keep it bright green). Set aside. This can be made up to 1 day in advance and refrigerated in a covered container.

Preheat the oven to 350°F.

To make the duck: Using a knife, score the duck skin on each breast, making a grid-like pattern. Place the breasts, skin-side down, in a large, heavy ovenproof skillet over medium heat. Sprinkle with salt and pepper. Slowly render the duck fat until the skin is crisp, about 10 minutes. Flip skin-side up, transfer to the oven, and finish cooking, about 6 minutes. Remove, cover loosely with foil, and allow to rest. Before serving, slice each breast on the diagonal into thin slices.

To make the mushrooms: While the duck is cooking, warm the canola oil in a large sauté pan over medium heat. Add the chanterelles and cook, tossing, until they begin to brown around the edges, about 5 minutes. Add the cooked spaetzle and continue to cook, tossing, until both mushrooms and spaetzle are crisp.

To serve, reheat the spinach purée in a small pan over low heat. Divide the spinach purée evenly among 4 plates, spooning some spaetzle on top of the purée. Arrange sliced duck breasts over the spaetzle and serve.

> **NEVER SAY NEVER PAIRING**
> The richness of this dish requires a luxury-level vintage Brut Champagne; recommended bottlings include Bollinger R.D., Roederer Cristal, and Krug Clos du Mesnil.

Grilled Mushroom and Citrus Salad with Bucheret

SERVES 6

This recipe is adapted from *Cooking One-on-One: Lessons from a Master Teacher* by John Ash. Any flavorful cultivated mushroom, such as shiitake, oyster, hen of the woods, portobello, and the like could be used. The mushrooms can also be broiled. For the dressing, Ash suggests using toasted hazelnut oil, though any fragrant, toasted nut oil—such as walnut, almond, or pecan—could be substituted.

SALAD

½ cup olive oil

2 tablespoons balsamic vinegar

2 teaspoons minced shallots

1 teaspoon fresh thyme, finely chopped

Salt and freshly ground black pepper

1½ pounds alba clamshell and baby oyster cluster mushrooms

8 cups lightly packed savory greens, such as a combination of frisée, arugula, and watercress

4 cups orange, grapefruit, or pomelo sections

½ cup hazelnuts or pecans, lightly toasted

6 ounces Bucheret cheese (see Note), sliced into 6 wedges

Savory sprouts, such as daikon, corn, lentil, or fenugreek, for garnish (optional)

VINAIGRETTE

⅓ cup toasted hazelnut oil

⅓ cup grapefruit juice

1 teaspoon brown sugar, or to taste

1 tablespoon finely chopped fresh mint

Drops of hot pepper sauce, to taste

Salt and freshly ground black pepper

SPECIAL EQUIPMENT: thin metal or wooden skewers, wooden skewers soaked in water for 30 minutes and drained

To prepare the mushrooms: Start a charcoal grill and build a moderately hot fire, or preheat a gas grill to medium. Whisk together the olive oil, balsamic vinegar, shallots, thyme, salt and pepper. Thread the mushrooms on the skewers and arrange on a baking sheet. Brush with the olive oil mixture and grill on both sides until tender and golden brown. Remove the mushrooms from the skewers and slice, if desired.

To make the vinaigrette: In a bowl, whisk the oil, grapefruit juice, and brown sugar together until the sugar is dissolved. Stir in the mint and add drops of hot sauce to taste; season with salt and pepper.

To finish the salad: In a large bowl, toss the greens with the vinaigrette and arrange on plates with the citrus, grilled mushrooms, toasted nuts, and cheese. Garnish each serving with sprouts, if using, and serve immediately.

NOTE: You can use any soft-ripened goat's-milk cheese you like, such as a French Bûcheron, but we suggest Redwood Hill Farm's Bucheret. Good cheese shops may carry it, or you can order directly at www.redwoodhill.com.

NEVER SAY NEVER PAIRING
Focus on the citrus in this multifaceted dish by serving it with a brut sparkling wine from the Pacific Northwest; recommended producers include Argyle from Oregon and Domaine Ste. Michelle from Washington.

Velveteen Corn Soup with Cornbread Croutons, Caviar, and Crème Fraîche

SERVES 4

With all its components, this soup is a study in contrasting flavors and textures: the sweetness of the corn and the cornbread, the saltiness of the caviar, the creaminess of both the soup and the crème fraîche. Of course fresh corn is preferred here, but this soup can also be made with frozen corn kernels. Powdered arrowroot, which is used as a thickener, is clear and tasteless when cooked.

4 slices cornbread, or 2 corn muffins, tops removed and bottoms sliced into 2 rounds each

3 cups fresh or frozen corn kernels (If using fresh corn, see Note)

3 cups whole milk

1 tablespoon butter

¼ teaspoon salt

⅛ teaspoon arrowroot

½ cup heavy cream

4 teaspoons sevruga caviar, or to taste

2½ tablespoons crème fraîche, or to taste

Fresh chives, chopped, for garnish

Ease of Preparation: Moderate

Preheat the oven to 250°F or set a toaster oven to the "toast" setting. Toast the sliced cornbread or muffins for 1 to 3 minutes, or just until the outside is slightly crusty, but not browned. (Watch carefully to make sure your muffins don't color too fast.) Set aside.

In a stockpot, heat the milk, corn, and cobs, if using, over medium heat for about 5 minutes, or until the mixture steams. To prevent scorching, immediately remove the pot from the heat. Remove and discard the cobs. Strain the milk and corn through a fine-mesh sieve into a large bowl, stirring and mashing the corn kernels to release their liquid. When you've mashed all you can, discard the kernels. Rinse out and dry the stockpot and strain the corn liquid back into it through the fine-mesh sieve. Repeat once more if necessary. The liquid should be completely smooth.

Return the stockpot to the heat and add the butter, salt, arrowroot, and cream. Stir to combine. Heat over medium heat for 1 to 1½ minutes, or until the mixture steams. Again, remove it immediately from the heat to prevent scorching. The butter should be melted and the mixture should be thickened slightly. (If not, let it sit for a minute off the heat.)

To serve, ladle the soup into bowls. Place a cornbread crouton in each bowl. Top each crouton with about 2 teaspoons crème fraîche and 1 teaspoon caviar. Sprinkle with chives. Serve immediately, while the soup is warm and the crème fraîche is cold.

NOTE: If you are using fresh corn, hold the shucked ears vertically over a cutting board and cut downward to remove the kernels from the cob. Don't throw away the cobs; cook them along with the kernels for a richer flavor.

PAIRING The creamy texture of a vintage or
nonvintage California brut mirrors the rich character
of this savory soup; recommended producers include
Schramsberg, Iron Horse, and Roederer Estate.
A less expensive alternative is Prosecco, from Italy.

Hearty Frittata with Potatoes, Red Pepper, Porcini Mushrooms, and Turkey Chorizo

SERVES 6 AS A MAIN COURSE

If you cannot find turkey chorizo, use andouille, or another zesty sausage. You can also use egg whites only, as opposed to whole eggs, for the base of the frittata.

3 tablespoons olive oil

1 large onion, cut into ¼-inch pieces

2 garlic cloves, finely chopped

2 medium russet potatoes, peeled and cut into bite-sized pieces

1 red bell pepper, cored, seeded, and cut into bite-sized pieces

4 ounces porcini or shiitake mushrooms, trimmed and sliced

Salt

2 links (about ¾ pound) turkey chorizo sausage, quartered and cut into ⅛-inch thick slices

10 to 12 eggs

¼ cup milk

½ to ¾ cup freshly grated Parmesan cheese, or a Parmesan-Romano blend

Ease of Preparation: Moderate

Pour the oil into a 12-inch nonstick ovenproof skillet, and tilt the pan to coat the bottom and sides. Heat the oil over medium-high heat until it ripples. Add the onion and garlic, stir to coat with the oil, and cook, stirring, for 7 to 10 minutes, or until the onions are translucent and softened.

Add the potatoes, toss to combine, and cook, stirring, for 5 minutes, or until the potatoes just begin to color. Add the bell pepper and cook, stirring, for about 3 minutes, or until softened. Add the mushrooms and cook, stirring, until they have exuded their liquid and it has evaporated. Add salt to taste.

Add the chorizo and cook, stirring, for about 4 minutes, or until browned. (If necessary, move the vegetables to the side of the skillet and move that side of the skillet off the heat to prevent them from sticking while the chorizo cooks.)

Preheat the oven to 350°F.

Beat 10 of the eggs in a large bowl until light yellow in color. Beat in the milk. Remove the skillet from the heat and pour the beaten eggs over the vegetables and chorizo. If there is not enough egg batter to come at least halfway up the sides of the ingredients in the skillet, beat the remaining 2 eggs and pour them over the ingredients to fill. (The vegetables and chorizo should not be completely submerged, but the surface should be fairly even.) Sprinkle the cheese over the frittata.

Cover the skillet and bake on the middle rack of the oven for 35 to 45 minutes, or until the eggs are cooked through and the potatoes can be easily pierced with the tip of a sharp knife. Ten to 15 minutes before the end of the cooking time, remove the cover to brown the cheese. Transfer the skillet to the table, cut the frittata into wedges, and serve from the skillet. Or let the frittata cool to room temperature and serve.

PAIRING For a festive brunch, serve this hearty frittata with a sparkling Shiraz from Australia or California; recommended wines include Barossa Valley Estate E&E (Australia) and Steele Black Bubbles (California).

Frozen Champagne Elderflower Soup with White Peaches

SERVES 8

This elegant dessert from Bill Yosses, White House Executive Pastry Chef under President George W. Bush, sounds complicated, but it's not hard if you have an ice cream maker. Elderflower syrup, basically a simple syrup infused with elderflowers and lemon juice, is available in some specialty stores and online.

¼ cups mineral water

1 bottle Champagne

2 ¼ cups elderflower syrup

¾ cup Muscat dessert wine, such as Beaumes de Venise or Quady Winery Essencia

3 ripe white peaches, halved, pitted, peeled, and cut into thin (⅛-inch) slices

SPECIAL EQUIPMENT: **4-inch round tart ring mold**

Ease of Preparation: Easy to Moderate

Combine all the liquids and freeze in an ice cream machine according to the manufacturer's instructions.

Place 8 soup bowls in the freezer 1 hour before needed.

To serve, place a 4-inch round tart ring mold in the bottom of one of the soup bowls. Fan a single layer of peach slices in the bottom of the mold. Using the back of a spoon, spread some of the sorbet into the mold and level it off with a spatula. Remove the mold, and garnish with a slice of white peach. Plate the remaining sorbet and sliced peaches in the same manner. Serve immediately.

PAIRING The various fruit elements of this dessert soup call for a slightly off-dry sparkling wine from France's Loire Valley; recommended producers include Langlois-Chateau and Bouvet-Ladubay.

Mediterranean Green Salad with Herbs and Fennel

SERVES 4 TO 6

This recipe, created by Michele Anna Jordan, is no everyday green salad. It combines two lettuces, plus scallions, fennel, toasted pine nuts, and no less than five fragrant, fresh herbs. Aptly named, it was inspired by salads from Sicily and the Greek Isles.

3 to 4 tablespoons extra virgin olive oil

2 tablespoons red wine vinegar

Freshly ground black pepper

1 head romaine lettuce, leaves separated, rinsed, and dried

1 head red leaf or butter lettuce, leaves separated, rinsed, and dried

1 medium fennel bulb, tough outer leaves removed, the bulb very thinly sliced

3 scallions, trimmed and very thinly sliced

3 tablespoons fresh mint leaves, thinly sliced

3 tablespoons fresh Italian parsley leaves, chopped

1 tablespoon chopped chives

1 teaspoon fresh oregano, minced (optional)

1 teaspoon fresh thyme, minced (optional)

Kosher salt

3 tablespoons pine nuts, toasted

Ease of Preparation: Easy

In a small bowl, whisk together the oil, vinegar, and plenty of pepper. Set aside.

Stack about a third of the lettuce leaves and roll them up lengthwise, then cut the lettuce roll crosswise into thin (about ⅜-inch) slices. Put the cut lettuce into a large salad bowl and repeat until all of the lettuce has been sliced.

Add the fennel, scallions, and all of the herbs to the bowl of lettuce, sprinkle with several generous pinches of salt, and toss gently. Pour the vinaigrette over the salad and gently toss to coat. Scatter the pine nuts over the top and serve immediately.

> **PAIRING** Garden herb freshness is the key to this pairing. Try a dry, clean Spanish Cava; recommended producers include Marqués de Monistrol, Codorníu, and Freixenet.

About Champagne and Sparkling Wines

The world of bubbly encompasses myriad styles and wines from around the globe: there's Champagne itself, Cava from Spain, Prosecco from Italy, Sekt from Germany, Cap Classique from South Africa, and a host of other traditional and more industrial sparklers.

Doubtless, Champagne is the most historic and high-reaching wine in the sparkling realm, hailing only from a denominated region in France of the same name. (Its boundaries, located about 90 miles northeast of Paris, were determined in 1927.)

Champagne's origins date back to the late seventeenth century, when, as so many wine books tell us, a monk named Pérignon stumbled upon a wine that had refermented in the bottle, causing him to embark on a path toward perfecting the method by which carbon dioxide bubbles could be deliberately added to still wines. Today, scientists have determined that approximately 50 million tiny bubbles exist in a typical bottle of Champagne.

By law, vintners in France may use three different varieties of grapes—Chardonnay, Pinot Noir, and Pinot Meunier—to make Champagne, with most Champagnes containing a portion of all three. The level of a Champagne's sweetness, which can range from ultra-crisp to downright sugary, is determined by what is known as the "dosage," which is a small amount of sugar and even a nip of brandy added to an almost-finished wine. The complexity and makeup of the dosage is what distinguishes one Champagne from another. Wines labeled "brut," which are dry and a bit savory, are the most common and also the most complex. Other types of Champagnes include extra dry and demi-sec (slightly sweet), sec (medium-dry), doux (the sweetest) and naturel (no dosage, thus crisp).

Bubbles can get into wine bottles in several ways. In the "traditional" method, or *méthode Champenoise*, a second fermentation takes place inside the bottle following the addition of additional sugar and yeasts. This is the process used by the world's best sparkling wines—Champagne, Cava, Franciacorta and various New World versions. French versions from outside Champagne often carry the word *crémant* as part of their names, such as *Crémant d'Alsace* or *Crémant de Bourgogne*. The *charmat* process also involves a second fermentation, but in a tank, with the bottling then performed under pressure; this is common in France's Loire Valley and in parts of Italy. At the bottom of the sparkling wine hierarchy, you will find wines that are carbonated in a way not dissimilar to how club soda is made.

Countries that produce traditional and charmat sparklers include France, Spain, Italy, Germany, Austria, England, Australia, South Africa, Chile, Argentina, Brazil, and the United States. Classic food pairings for Champagne and sparkling wines include oysters and other shellfish, caviar, nuts and olives, lobster, baked fish, hard cheeses, and chocolate. But in truth, the possibilities are almost endless.

Chapter 7

Fortified &
Dessert Wines

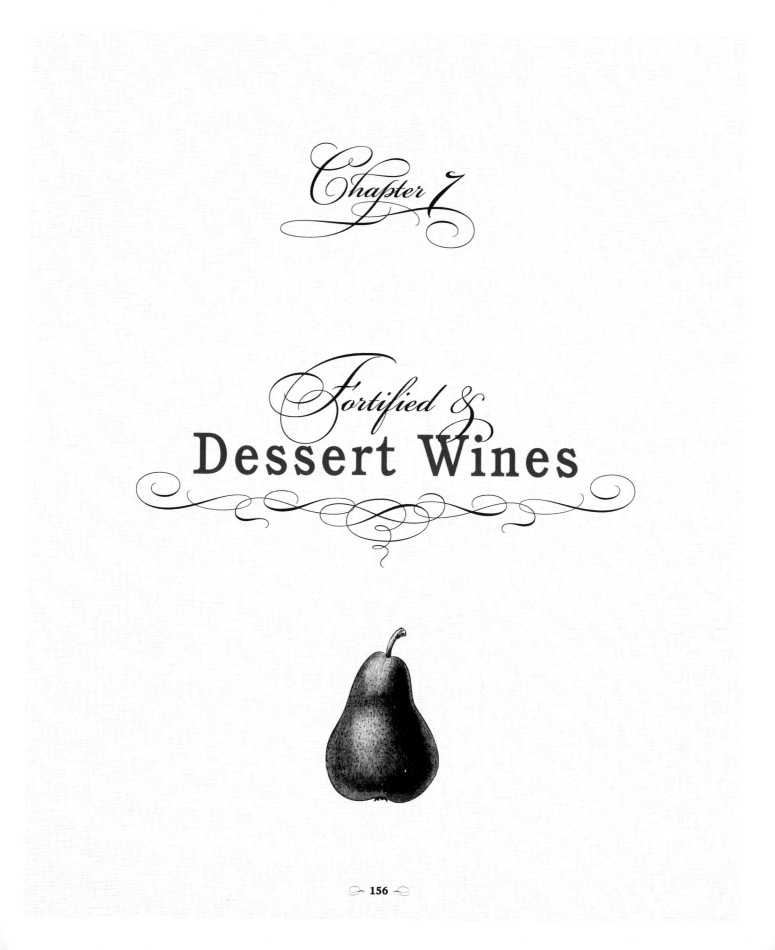

If you are a dessert lover—and who isn't?—you've come to the right chapter. Here's another treat: the pairing guidelines for these wines couldn't be easier or clearer. Dessert wines go with desserts—that's it. And, although less obvious from a linguistic point of view, so do fortified wines. Of the thirteen recipes that follow, eight are desserts, ranging from pears poached in Armagnac to authentic Italian biscotti to Catalan flan with bay leaf fritters to two glorious cakes. Chocolate recipes figure prominently, too, because Port, a fortified wine, is *the* classic match with chocolate. Which will you make first? Will it be the chocolate soufflés (page 164), a bittersweet chocolate cake (page 166), or perhaps chocolate pecan pie bars (page 162)? The decision itself is delicious.

Less predictable—and perhaps more intriguing for that reason—are the savory recipes that we've paired with dessert wines: Roquefort Shortbreads (page 175) and Asparagus with Foie Gras in Phyllo Packages (page 171). Like the desserts mentioned above, these hors d'oeuvres are celebratory in a keynote kind of way, and both are paired with celebratory wines—Sauternes or Barsac—that are perfect matches with the main ingredients, Roquefort (blue) cheese and foie gras.

There are also savory options among the recipes that are paired with fortified wines. Sherry lovers, listen up: Chorizo and Shrimp with Palo Cortado (page 159) are paired with the same palo cortado Sherry that figures so predominantly in the sauce for this Spanish combination; BBQ Duck–Filled Blue Corn Pancakes with Habañero Sauce are paired with a Mosel Riesling auslese, and, last but hardly least, a Wild Mushroom and Tomato Risotto (page 174), our Never Say Never, is matched with a dry Oloroso Sherry.

Savory or sweet, fortified or dessert—you'll find intriguing options and unexpected discoveries in the selection of recipes that follow.

Chorizo and Shrimp with Palo Cortado

MAKES 8 SKEWERS

Sherry, the famed wine from the southwestern tip of Spain, imparts a lovely richness to cooking. The following recipe calls for palo cortado Sherry, a rare form of dry Sherry that has hazelnut aromas of amontillado Sherry and the rich, dark color and almost nutty flavor of oloroso Sherry. It works beautifully with food. If you can't find it, an oloroso or amontillado will work, too.

2 tablespoons olive oil

2 large shallots, thinly sliced

1 pound Spanish chorizo sausage, sliced into ⅓-inch rounds

1¼ cups dry red wine

¼ cup palo cortado Sherry

4 bay leaves

8 sprigs fresh thyme

2 tablespoons chili oil

16 large shrimp, peeled and deveined

1 loaf crusty bread, for serving

Fresh flat-leaf parsley, chopped, for garnish

SPECIAL EQUIPMENT: small metal or wooden skewers, for serving

Ease of Preparation: Easy to Moderate

In a large skillet, heat the oil over medium-high heat until it ripples. Add the shallots and cook, stirring, until tender and translucent, about 5 minutes. Using a slotted spoon, remove the shallots from the pan; set aside. Add the chorizo to the skillet and sauté, stirring, until lightly browned. Add the red wine, Sherry, bay leaves, thyme, and reserved shallots. Simmer until the wine is reduced in volume and slightly thickened, about 5 minutes. Remove the pan from the heat and cover loosely with foil to keep warm.

In another large skillet, heat the chili oil until hot. Add the shrimp in one layer and sauté quickly, stirring, until pink and firm. Do not overcook.

Thread the shrimp and chorizo slices onto skewers, alternating them and allowing 2 shrimp per skewer. Arrange the skewers on a serving platter. Slice the bread and arrange on another serving platter.

Remove the bay leaves and thyme sprigs from the sauce, drizzle the sauce over the skewers, and garnish with the parsley. Serve immediately, with the bread as an accompaniment.

> **PAIRING** Pair this easy dish with the same Palo Cortado used in the recipe; recommended Palo Cortados include Lustau Peninsula, and Sanchez Romate Regente.

BBQ Duck–Filled Blue Corn Pancakes with Habañero Sauce

SERVES 8

From Chef Bobby Flay's celebrated *Bobby Flay's Mesa Grill Cookbook*, this recipe features a tantalizing combination of sweetness and spice, with blue corn pancakes enveloping sumptuous duck that has been baked in barbecue and habañero sauce.

MESA BBQ SAUCE

2 tablespoons canola oil

1 large Spanish onion, coarsely chopped

5 cloves garlic, coarsely chopped

3 cups canned plum tomatoes and juices, puréed

1 cup water

¼ cup ketchup

¼ cup red wine vinegar

¼ cup Worcestershire sauce

3 tablespoons Dijon mustard

3 tablespoons dark brown sugar

2 tablespoon honey

¼ cup molasses

3 tablespoons ancho chile powder

3 tablespoons pasilla chile powder

2 tablespoons puréed chipotle chiles in adobo

Salt and freshly ground pepper

DUCK

6 duck legs, skin removed

3 cups chicken stock

Sautéed shiitake mushrooms

3 tablespoons coarsely chopped cilantro

Salt and freshly ground pepper

HABAÑERO SAUCE

10 cups chicken stock

1 cup apple juice concentrate, thawed

3 tablespoons dark brown sugar

2 star anise

1 cinnamon stick

½ habañero pepper, coarsely chopped

1 tablespoon fennel seeds, toasted

Salt and freshly ground pepper

PANCAKES

½ cup blue cornmeal

½ cup all-purpose flour

1 teaspoon baking powder

Pinch of salt

1 large egg, beaten

¾ cup whole milk

2 tablespoons honey

1 tablespoon unsalted butter, melted

Ease of Preparation: Moderate to Difficult

To make the barbecue sauce: Heat the oil in a heavy-bottomed medium saucepan over medium-high heat. Add the onion and cook until soft, 3 to 4 minutes. Add the garlic and cook for 1 minute. Add the tomatoes and water, bring to a boil, and simmer for 10 minutes. Add the remaining ingredients and simmer for an additional 30 to 40 minutes until thickened, stirring occasionally.

Transfer the mixture to a food processor and purée until smooth; season with salt and pepper to taste. Pour into a bowl and allow to cool to room temperature. (This sauce will keep for 1 week in the refrigerator stored in a tightly sealed container.)

To make the duck: Preheat oven to 325°F. Generously brush the duck legs with the BBQ Sauce and place them in a baking pan. Pour the stock and ½ cup of the Habañero Sauce around them. Cover the pan and cook for 2 hours or until the meat begins to fall off the bone.

Meanwhile, make the habañero sauce: Place all of the ingredients in a large saucepan over high heat and cook until the mixture reduces to 1 ½ cups, after about 1 ½ hours, stirring occasionally. Strain into a bowl and season with salt and pepper to taste.

When the duck is cooked, remove it from the braising liquid and let it cool slightly. Strain the braising liquid and reserve. When the duck is cool enough to handle, shred the duck meat into bite-size pieces and discard the bones. Place the duck meat, mushrooms, and ½ cup of the BBQ braising liquid in a sauté pan and cook over medium heat until heated through. Add the cilantro and season with salt and pepper.

To make the pancakes: Combine the cornmeal, flour, baking powder, and salt in a medium bowl. In a separate bowl, combine the egg, milk, honey, and butter. Add the wet ingredients to the dry ingredients and mix until combined.

Place a 6-inch nonstick pan over high heat. Spray the pan with cooking spray and reduce the heat to medium. Ladle 2 ounces of the pancake batter into the pan, swirling to evenly coat the pan. Cook the pancake until just set on the first side, about 1 minute. Flip the pancake over and cook for an additional 20 to 30 seconds. Remove to a plate and repeat all steps with the remaining mixture, stacking the pancakes and covering them with foil to keep warm.

To assemble the pancakes, mound some of the duck mixture in the center of each pancake. Fold the pancake over the filling to make a semi-circle and drizzle with the remaining Habañero Sauce. Garnish with chopped cilantro.

> **PAIRING** Although they have considerable residual sugar, many German auslesen also have enough acidity to pair comfortably with savory dishes. In combination with the wine's modest alcohol levels, a Mosel Riesling auslese from a good producer, such as Dr. Loosen or Grans-Fassian, will complement this recipe's marriage of sweetness and spice.

Frontera's Chocolate Pecan Pie Bars

MAKES 24 BARS

This recipe is adapted from Rick Bayless's *Salsas That Cook*. An authority on traditional Mexican cooking, Rick Bayless is a Chicago chef and restaurateur, Frontera Grill being one of his renowned eateries. For these bars, Bayless recommends that you line your baking pan with a carefully flattened piece of heavy-duty aluminum foil to help remove them from the pan. Chilling the bars after baking will make them easier to cut.

2½ cups (about 10 ounces) pecan halves

1 cup (about 6 ounces) finely chopped Mexican chocolate (such as Ibarra)

6 ounces (about 6 to 8 slices) fresh white bread, preferably cakey sandwich bread, broken into large pieces

1 cup (2 sticks) butter, melted

Generous ¾ teaspoon salt

5 ounces semisweet or bittersweet chocolate, chopped into pieces not larger than ¼ inch

3 tablespoons all-purpose flour

4 large eggs

1 cup packed dark brown sugar

1 cup dark corn syrup (or you can use a mixture of corn syrup and molasses, sorghum, or Steen's cane syrup)

2 teaspoons pure vanilla extract

Powdered sugar, for garnish

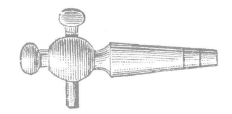

Preheat the oven to 325°F.

Spread the pecans on a baking sheet. Bake until richly browned and toasty, about 10 minutes. Maintain oven temperature. Let the pecans cool, then scoop them into a food processor and coarsely chop by pulsing the machine on and off. Transfer about 1½ cups of the nuts to a large bowl to use in the filling.

Add half of the Mexican chocolate to the nuts in the processor and pulse the machine to mix. Add the bread; process until everything is chopped to fairly fine crumbs. Add ⅓ cup of the melted butter and ¼ teaspoon of the salt. Process just to moisten everything. Liberally butter a 13 x 9-inch baking pan, then pat the crumb crust mixture evenly into the buttered pan. Refrigerate the crust while you make the filling.

Add the remaining Mexican chocolate, the chopped semisweet chocolate, and the flour to the bowl with the reserved pecans.

In a food processor (you don't even need to clean it), mix the eggs and sugar until well-combined. Add the corn syrup, pulse a couple of times, then add the remaining ⅔ cup melted butter, the remaining ½ teaspoon salt, and the vanilla. Process to combine thoroughly. Pour the egg mixture over the pecan-filling mixture in the bowl, stir well, and scrape into the crust-lined pan, making an even layer.

Bake 40 to 50 minutes, or until the bars have pulled away slightly from the sides of the pan. Let cool to room temperature (and chill, if desired) before cutting into 2-inch squares.

To serve, sprinkle the pie bars with powdered sugar and arrange them on a serving platter.

PAIRING A classic pairing of like with like: Pair the sweetness and spice in this chocolate dessert with a sweet, spicy LBV (Late-Bottled Vintage) Port; recommended producers include Fonseca, Warre's and Ramos-Pinto.

Warm Chocolate Soufflés

SERVES 2

This recipe is adapted from François Payard's *Simply Sensational Desserts*. Payard is one of New York's foremost pastry chefs. He notes that while many chocolate soufflés are made with cocoa powder, the best, most luxuriant ones require real chocolate (as in the recipe below).

¾ tablespoon unsalted butter, cut into ½-inch cubes, plus more for ramekins

4 teaspoons sugar, plus more for ramekins

1 ¾ ounces bittersweet chocolate, chopped

1 large egg, separated, at room temperature

1 large egg white, at room temperature

⅛ teaspoon cream of tartar

Pistachio ice cream, for serving (optional)

PAIRING The sweetness of this soufflé contrasts well with the nutty caramel quality of a Tawny Port or Banyuls; recommended Tawny Ports include Dow's 30-year; Taylor Fladgate 20-year and Niepoort 10-year; a recommended Banyuls producer is M. Chapoutier.

Ease of Preparation: Moderate

Generously butter the insides of two 6- or 8-ounce ramekins. Chill the ramekins in the freezer for 15 minutes. Butter the ramekins again, dust the insides with sugar, and tap out the excess. Return the ramekins to the refrigerator while you make the soufflé base.

Fill a medium saucepan one-third full with water and bring to a simmer. Place the chocolate and the ¾ tablespoon butter in a medium heatproof bowl, set the bowl over the simmering water, and melt, stirring occasionally, until completely smooth. Remove the bowl from the pan and set aside to cool.

Preheat the oven to 350°F.

Whisk the egg yolk into the cooled chocolate mixture until smooth.

In a clean, dry bowl, beat the egg white with an electric mixer on low speed until foamy. Add the cream of tartar, increase the speed to medium-high, and beat until soft peaks form. Gradually add the 4 teaspoons sugar and beat on high speed until stiff peaks form. Using a large rubber spatula, fold 1 mound of the beaten egg whites into the chocolate mixture, then gently fold in the remaining beaten whites.

Spoon the mixture into the chilled prepared ramekins, filling each about three-quarters full. Run your thumb around the inside edge of each ramekin, wiping off the sugar and butter from the rim.

Place the ramekins on a baking sheet and bake for 11 to 13 minutes, until puffed. Serve immediately. If you wish, crack the top of each soufflé with the back of a spoon and top with a scoop of pistachio ice cream.

Warm Chocolate Cakes with Dulce De Leche

SERVES: 6

From Pastry Chef Vicki Wells of Bobby Flay's Mesa Grill, these delectable chocolate cakes feature dulce de leche, the tremendously popular caramel sauce introduced to Americans by Latin chefs. Chocolate and caramel flavor every bite, for a magnificent treat.

DULCE DE LECHE

1 cup whole milk

1 cup unsweetened coconut milk

1 cup goat's milk

2½ tablespoons dark corn syrup

¼ cup sugar

2 canella cinnamon sticks

1 vanilla bean

¼ teaspoon baking soda

CAKES

¼ pound (1 stick) unsalted butter, plus more for molds

1 tablespoon all-purpose flour, plus more for molds

4 ounces bittersweet chocolate, chopped

2 large eggs

2 large eggs, separated

¼ cup sugar

GARNISH

Vanilla or pecan ice cream

Hot fudge sauce

Ease of Preparation: Easy to Moderate

To make the Dulce de Leche: Place the milks, corn syrup, sugar, cinnamon sticks, and vanilla bean in a medium saucepan and bring to a boil.

Dissolve the baking soda in small bowl with a little water and whisk into the milk mixture. Cook the mixture, stirring occasionally, until reduced by half and caramelized. Transfer the mixture to a bowl and place it in the refrigerator until chilled and firm. (This will keep, tightly covered, in the refrigerator for about 1 week.)

To make the cakes: Preheat the oven to 425°F. Butter and lightly flour six 4-ounce ramekins or custard cups. Tap out excess flour; butter and flour them again; set aside.

Place the butter and chocolate in the top of a double boiler or heat-proof bowl set over a pan of simmering water, and heat until the chocolate has completely melted. Remove from the heat and let cool slightly.

In the bowl of an electric mixer fitted with the paddle attachment, beat together the 2 eggs, 2 egg yolks, and sugar until light and thick. Add the melted chocolate and beat to combine. Quickly beat in the flour until just combined.

In another bowl of an electric mixer, whip the 2 egg whites until soft peaks form, then fold them into the chocolate mixture. Fill each ramekin half way with the batter. Place a tablespoon of dulce de leche in the center and top with the remaining batter. Place the filled molds on a baking sheet, and bake until the sides have set but the centers remain soft, about 6 to 7 minutes.

Invert each mold onto a plate, and let rest 10 seconds. Unmold the cakes by running a small knife around the perimeter of the cakes and slightly lifting up one edge of the cake; the cake will fall out onto the plate. Serve with ice cream and hot fudge sauce.

> **PAIRING** A rich gooey dessert deserves a rich gooey wine, like a Malmsey Madeira. Try a 5-year-old Malmsey from Blandy's or Cossart-Gordon; the delicate nuances of an older wine might be overwhelmed by the dish.

Spiced-Rum Cake with Caramel-Rum Frosting and Candied Walnuts

MAKES ONE 9-INCH 2-LAYER CAKE; SERVES 8 TO 10

This rich, full-flavored spice cake is well worth the effort (and time) it takes to make. Not incidentally, the candied walnuts are delicious on their own. Make a batch of them for snacking on, sprinkling over ice cream, or for decorating other desserts. Note that the frosting is based on classic caramel sauce and, as such, you should exercise caution when working with the hot sugar—get out the long-handled wooden spoon and thick potholders.

CANDIED WALNUTS

1½ cups walnut halves (about 6 ounces)

2 tablespoons sugar

2 tablespoons light or dark brown sugar

Pinch of salt

4 tablespoons unsalted butter, cut into pieces

4 teaspoons dark rum

FROSTING

1¼ cups sugar

½ teaspoon fresh lemon juice

2 cups heavy cream

2 tablespoons dark rum

CAKE

2½ cups all-purpose flour

2 teaspoons ground cinnamon

1 teaspoon baking soda

¾ teaspoon ground cloves

¾ teaspoon freshly grated nutmeg

½ teaspoon baking powder

½ teaspoon salt

½ teaspoon ground ginger

½ teaspoon allspice

1 cup milk

¼ cup dark rum

½ cup (1 stick) unsalted butter, at room temperature

½ cup sugar

½ cup packed light or dark brown sugar

2 large eggs

1 cup chopped walnuts (about 4 ounces)

Preheat the oven to 350°F.

To make the candied walnuts: In a bowl, toss the walnut halves with both sugars and the salt. Spread the walnuts in a single layer in a shallow roasting pan just large enough to hold them. Scatter the pieces of butter over the nuts and sprinkle with the rum. Roast for 10 to 12 minutes, or until golden brown, stirring the nuts and shaking the pan 2 or 3 times during roasting. For darker nuts, roast for an additional 2 to 3 minutes. Spread the nuts on a plate or tray to cool and use right away, or store them in an airtight container at room temperature for up to 3 days.

To make the cake: Position an oven rack in the center of the oven. Preheat the oven to 350°F. Butter and lightly flour the bottom and sides of two 9-inch round cake pans. Cut a piece of parchment or wax paper to fit in the bottoms of the pans. Insert the paper rounds and butter and lightly flour them.

In a large bowl, whisk together the flour, cinnamon, baking soda, cloves, nutmeg, baking powder, salt, ginger and allspice. In a glass measuring cup or bowl, stir together the milk and rum.

In the bowl of an electric mixer fitted with the paddle attachment, cream the butter and both sugars on medium-high speed until light and fluffy. Add the eggs, one at a time, beating well after each one. Reduce the mixer to medium-low and add some of the milk mixture, alternating with some of the flour mixture, until well combined. Stir in the chopped walnuts.

Using a rubber spatula, scrape the batter into the prepared pans, dividing it evenly between them. Smooth the surface of the pans and bake for 25 to 30 minutes, or until a toothpick inserted into the center of the layers comes out clean and the cakes spring back when gently pressed and pull away from the sides of the pan. Let the cakes cool in their pans on wire racks for 10 minutes. Turn the cakes out onto the racks and let them cool completely.

To make the frosting: Fill a large bowl with ice cubes and water. Set aside.

In a large, heavy saucepan, combine the sugar, water, and lemon juice and cook over medium-high heat for 8 to 10 minutes, or until the mixture turns amber. Stir this mixture for the first 2 minutes with a wooden spoon but once the sugar melts, stop stirring and only tilt the pan to ensure even cooking. Take care; *the sugar is very hot*. (If the sugar burns, turns dark, and smells acrid, discard it and start again.)

Remove the pan from the heat and slowly and carefully pour ½ cup of the cream into the pan. It will bubble and foam. Stir with a long-handled wooden spoon until the bubbling subsides and the mixture is blended and smooth. Add the rum and stir well.

Transfer the caramel-cream mixture to the bowl of an electric mixer fitted with the whisk attachment and beat for about 5 minutes, or until the caramel lightens in color and thickens further. Scrape into a small bowl and set aside.

In a clean bowl of the electric mixer fitted with the whisk attachment and set on medium-high speed, beat the remaining 1½ cups of cream until stiff. Add the reserved caramel to the cream and whip just until blended and the frosting is spreadable. The caramel will deflate the whipped cream but it will hold its body. Do not overbeat or the frosting will separate. Refrigerate the frosting for up to 30 minutes until needed.

Meanwhile, in the bowl of a food processor fitted with the metal blade, process about two-thirds of the candied walnuts until coarsely ground. Reserve the best-looking, largest walnuts to decorate the cake.

Trim the cake layers with a long, serrated knife to ensure they are even. Put one layer on a cake plate and spread frosting over the top of the cake layer. Sprinkle with about a third of the ground walnuts and using the back of a spoon or a rubber spatula, gently press the nuts into the frosting.

Top with the remaining cake layer. Using a long, metal spatula, spread the rest of the frosting over the top and around the sides of the cake. Decorate the top and sides of the cake with the remaining chopped walnuts and the reserved whole walnuts halves.

Asparagus in Foie Gras Phyllo Packages

MAKES 12 APPETIZERS

One of the most difficult wines for Americans to pair with hors d'oeuvres is Sauternes. It is always thought of as an after-dinner or dessert drink, but it is actually best served as an apéritif with small bites, particularly anything containing blue cheese or foie gras, as in these savory phyllo "packages." This recipe was created by Bordeaux chef and restaurateur Georges Gotrand.

12 thin spears green asparagus, trimmed and scraped

2 ounces mousse de foie gras

10 basil leaves, chopped

½ teaspoon olive oil

6 sheets frozen phyllo dough, thawed

5 generous tablespoons butter, melted

Ease of Preparation: Moderate

Preheat the oven to 375°F.

In a large skillet, bring salted water to a boil. Add the asparagus and cook 5 to 7 minutes, until tender when pierced with a fork. Drain the asparagus, rinse under cold running water, and set aside on paper towels to drain.

In a large bowl, combine the mousse de foie gras, basil, and olive oil.

Place one sheet of the phyllo dough on a clean, dry work surface, and brush lightly with some of the melted butter. Repeat with two more sheets, stacking each on top of the first.

Spread half of the mousse mixture over the top sheet of dough, then cut it into 6 equal squares. Place 1 asparagus spear on each of the 6 squares, leaving a ½ inch of pastry on the bottom. Fold the dough on the bottom over the asparagus base, then fold each side over and pinch to create a purse-like seal. Repeat with the remaining squares in the same manner, then repeat using the remaining sheets of phyllo, butter, mousse mixture, and asparagus spears to create 6 more squares.

Place the asparagus packages on a baking sheet, brush lightly with more of the melted butter, and bake for 10 to 12 minutes, until lightly browned. Transfer the pastries to a serving platter and serve while still warm.

> **PAIRING** Focus on the richness of the foie gras by pairing with a similarly unctuous Sauternes or Barsac: recommended producers include Château Suduiraut, Château Riussec, and Château Nairac (Barsac).

Pears Poached in Armagnac
with Vanilla Ice Cream

SERVES 6 TO 8

Armagnac's pungent taste makes for a delicious poaching liquid and sauce.

2 cinnamon sticks, cut in half

2 vanilla beans, halved lengthwise

1 cup brown sugar

2 cups VSOP Armagnac

6 pears, halved lengthwise and cored

Vanilla ice cream, slightly softened, for serving

Ginger cookies, for serving

Ease of Preparation: Easy

In a 2-quart saucepan, combine 1¼ cups water (preferably still mineral water) with the cinnamon sticks, vanilla beans, sugar, and Armagnac and cook over medium heat until the sugar dissolves.

Add the halved pears. Simmer for 15 to 20 minutes, stirring frequently but gently, until the pears are tender. Remove from the heat; carefully transfer the pears and sauce to a bowl. Cover and refrigerate for at least 4 hours.

When ready to serve, remove the bowl from the refrigerator. Using a slotted spoon, transfer the pear halves to another bowl; remove the vanilla beans and cinnamon bits. Strain the remaining liquid over the pears.

Spoon the ice cream into individual serving dishes. Divide the pears among the dishes. Drizzle some of the sauce over each serving and garnish with ginger cookies.

PAIRING Wine lovers may pair this with a rich Monbazillac from southwest Frances, but spirits drinkers may want to serve this with an XO Armagnac. Recommended producers include Francis Darroze, Château de Laubade, and Château du Busca.

Wild Mushroom and Tomato Risotto

SERVES 6

This sophisticated risotto is great as a starter or side dish with roasted meat or poultry, but it can also serve as a stylish vegetarian entrée. Be creative with your choice of mushrooms in this dish— porcini, morels, chanterelles, or shiitakes are all superb options.

¾ cup olive oil

¾ pound fresh wild mushrooms, trimmed and finely chopped

3 shallots, diced

¾ cup dry white wine, such as Sauvignon Blanc

¾ pound risotto rice

6 cups vegetable stock

3 medium tomatoes, diced

2 tablespoons chopped fresh basil and chives

3 tablespoons mascarpone cheese

¼ cup grated Parmesan cheese

Salt and freshly ground black pepper

Fresh chervil sprigs, for garnish

Ease of Preparation: Moderate

Heat 3 tablespoons of the olive oil in a sauté pan over high heat, add the mushrooms, and sauté for 3 to 5 minutes, until they caramelize. Transfer the mushrooms to a plate and cover to keep warm.

In the same pan, heat the remaining oil, add the shallots, and sauté for 3 to 5 minutes, or until they soften. Add the wine and cook until it reduces, 3 to 5 minutes. Add the rice and stir to coat. Add 1 cup of stock and stir, allowing the rice to almost completely absorb in the stock. Continue adding the stock, 1 cup at a time, and stirring after each addition. Wait until the stock is mostly absorbed by the rice before adding the next cup of stock. Eventually, the rice will achieve a creamy consistency, and the grains should be just al dente—soft but still a bit crunchy.

Stir in the mushrooms, tomatoes, herbs, mascarpone, half the Parmesan cheese, and salt and pepper to taste.

To serve, transfer the risotto to a serving dish, sprinkle with the remaining Parmesan, and garnish with chervil sprigs.

> **NEVER SAY NEVER PAIRING**
> The rich earthiness of the wild mushrooms give this risotto the weight to stand up to a dry Oloroso Sherry; recommended producers include González Byass and Lustau.

Roquefort Shortbread

MAKES 12 APPETIZERS

Bordeaux chef and restaurateur Georges Gotrand created these bite-size appetizers. The dough can be made up to one day in advance and kept in the refrigerator until ready to be cut and baked. These are memorable served while still warm and are particularly good for holiday entertaining.

½ cup (1 stick) unsalted butter, at room temperature

6 ounces Roquefort cheese

2¼ cups all-purpose flour

1 egg yolk

Ease of Preparation: Easy

Using an electric mixer, cream the butter and cheese until well blended. Beat in the flour and egg yolk until combined. Divide the dough in half, then roll each half into a log 1½ inches in diameter. Wrap each log in plastic wrap and chill until firm.

Preheat the oven to 375°F.

Using a sharp knife, cut each log into ¼-inch slices, and place the rounds on a baking sheet, leaving 1 inch of space between rounds. Bake for 10 to 12 minutes, or until golden brown. Serve the shortbread hot or cold.

PAIRING Roquefort and Sauternes is a classic pairing—the sweet opulence of a Sauternes complements the salty tang of the cheese. Try with a Sauternes or Barsac; recommended producers include Château Doisy-Daëne, Château Filhot, Château Lafaurie-Peyraguey, and Château Coutet (Barsac).

Crema Catalana with Bay Leaf Buñuelos

SERVES 8, MAKES 8 CUSTARDS AND 48 FRITTERS

In this matchup, *buñuelos*, what Spaniards call doughnuts or fritters, provide Catalan-inspired flan with a crunchy, sweet sidekick. Andy Nusser, chef and co-owner of Casa Mono in New York City, has chosen to form his *buñuelos* around fresh bay leaves, which turn crackly when fried— an ingenious touch. Not surprisingly, this dessert wowed judges at the Second Annual Copa Jeréz, a food-and-Sherry pairings competition held in 2007 in Jeréz, Spain. The first bite is all sugar and addictively crisp batter. The inside, however, is mildly herbal and undeniably satisfying. For a touch of authenticity, make these in individual *cazuelas*, Spain's beautiful terra cotta cooking vessels. If you don't have *cazuelas*, ovenproof ramekins will work as well.

CUSTARD

1 quart (4 cups) heavy cream

1 cinnamon stick

1 vanilla bean

8 egg yolks

1 cup sugar, plus additional for sprinkling

4 sheets gelatin

SPECIAL EQUIPMENT: **kitchen blowtorch**

BUÑUELOS

6 cups all-purpose flour

3 cups sugar, plus additional for sprinkling

4 cups milk

3 egg whites, whipped to soft peaks

2 quarts extra virgin olive oil

4 dozen fresh bay leaves

SPECIAL EQUIPMENT: **deep-fat (or candy) thermometer**

Ease of Preparation: Moderate to Difficult

To make the custard: Preheat the oven to 325°F. Place 8 individual dessert-sized *cazuelas* or ovenproof ramekins in a heavy roasting pan that is large enough to hold them all without touching.

In a saucepan, heat the cream with the cinnamon stick and vanilla bean over medium heat until it is almost at a boil. Meanwhile, in a large bowl, whisk the egg yolks and sugar until smooth.

When the cream is almost at the boiling point, add the gelatin, one sheet at a time, directly to the cream, stirring constantly. Pour half of the hot cream into the large bowl with the egg yolk and sugar mixture, whisking together. Pour the yolk-cream mixture back into the saucepan of remaining heated cream and "cook" while stirring with a wooden spoon. At this point you should be achieving a nap, where the back of the spoon is coated with the custard. Do not overcook; turn the heat off if necessary. (At this stage, you are only melding the cream, egg yolks, sugar, and gelatin together.)

Strain the mixture through a fine-mesh strainer into a large bowl, pressing the vanilla bean against the strainer to extract the fullest flavor.

Pour the mixture into a pitcher, then fill each baking dish three-quarters full. Carefully add enough cold water to the roasting pan to reach halfway up the sides of the ramekins, then cover the pan with aluminum foil. Bake for 35 minutes. Remove the foil to check for a skin layer on the custards, which indicates that the custard has set. Remove the baking dishes to a rack and let cool. When cool, sprinkle some sugar over the tops of the custards and using a kitchen blowtorch, caramelize the sugar.

To make the buñuelos: In a large bowl, stir together the flour and sugar. Whisk in the milk until combined. Fold in the egg whites.

In a large, deep-sided pot, heat the olive oil to 360°F on a deep-fat thermometer. Dip the bay leaves in the batter and coat liberally. Delicately place the battered leaves in the hot oil and fry until golden all over. Using a slotted spoon, transfer the fritters to paper towels to drain and cool. When cool, sprinkle the fritters with sugar. Serve 6 *buñeulos* with each custard.

PAIRING The crunchy sweetness of the *buñuelos* pair well with the delicate flavor and the unctuous mouthfeel of a Moscatel-based sweet wine from southern Spain; recommended wines include Jorge Ordoñez & Co. Old Vines and Vinos de Telmo Rodríguez Molino Real Mountain Wine.

White Chocolate Rice Pudding

SERVES 4 TO 6

Italy's renowned Arborio rice, a short-grained variety, is best known as the rice of choice for risotto. It works in this elegant rice pudding, as well, which was originally contributed by pastry chef Mimi Young of Scala's Bistro in San Francisco.

RICE

4 cups whole milk

⅓ cup sugar

1 vanilla bean, split in half lengthwise

½ teaspoon salt

1 cup Arborio rice

CUSTARD

1 cup whole milk

1 cup heavy cream

2 large eggs

2 egg yolks

1 tablespoon dark rum

1 teaspoon pure vanilla extract

9 ounces white chocolate, finely chopped

1 cup heavy cream, whipped to soft peaks

NEVER SAY NAVER PAIRING

The rich mouthfeel of this pudding needs a rich wine to keep up. Try an Australian Muscat; recommended producers include Campbells, De Bortoli, and Chambers Rosewood Vineyards. A tawny Port would also make a comfortable match.

Ease of Preparation: Moderate

To make the rice: Place the milk, sugar, vanilla bean, and salt in a large, heavy saucepan and bring to a boil. Reduce the heat to low and stir in the rice. Simmer, partially covered, for about 25 minutes, or until 90 percent of the liquid has been absorbed, stirring occasionally. The rice should be firm but completely cooked. Remove the pan from the heat and let the rice rest, covered, for about 10 minutes. Discard the vanilla bean.

To make the custard: Place the milk and cream in a saucepan and bring to a boil. In a small bowl, whisk together the eggs and yolks. Add a bit of the hot milk mixture to the eggs, whisking quickly to temper the eggs. Pour the tempered egg mixture into the hot milk mixture while whisking. Whisk in the rum and vanilla. Pour the mixture over the rice and stir to combine.

Preheat the oven to 350°F. Grease a medium baking dish or soufflé dish.

Scrape the rice mixture into the prepared baking dish and cover with foil. Place the dish in a larger baking pan and fill the larger pan with enough very hot tap water to reach halfway up the sides of the rice pudding dish. Bake the pudding for 45 minutes, stirring the mixture every 15 minutes. The custard should be just barely set, but still creamy.

Remove the dish from the water bath and stir in the white chocolate. Press a piece of plastic film onto the surface of the pudding to prevent a skin from forming. Cool to room temperature, then refrigerate for at least 2 hours.

Before serving, fold whipped cream into the chilled pudding to lighten the texture to the desired consistency. Serve with the remaining whipped cream, if desired.

Tuscany's Cantucci

MAKES ABOUT 24 TO 30 COOKIES

The Antonio Mattei cookie factory in Prato, Tuscany, has been making one product since its founding in 1858: dried biscuits called *cantucci*, or "*biscotti di Prato*." (In America, we refer to them as "biscotti.") A genuine Tuscan meal always ends with a glass of vin santo and a plate of *cantucci*. The cookies are dipped into the wine quickly so that they absorb its sweet aromas and a superficial coating of moisture, but maintain crunchiness in the mouth.

4 cups all-purpose flour

2 cups sugar

4 eggs

1 teaspoon baking powder

1 cup almonds with skins

⅓ cup pine nuts

Pinch of salt

Ease of Preparation: Moderate

Preheat the oven to 360°F. Line a large baking sheet with parchment paper.

In a large bowl, stir together the flour and sugar. Stir in the eggs until combined, then add the remaining ingredients. Roll the dough into a ball.

On a clean work surface, shape the dough into 1-inch ribbons as long as your baking sheet and arrange them on the prepared baking sheet. Lightly flatten the tops of the rolls. Bake for 30 minutes. While the rolls are still warm but firm, cut them into ½-inch-wide slices.

Turn the slices on one side, making sure that the slices don't touch. Reduce the oven temperature to 250°F and bake the cookies on their sides for 10 minutes. Turn the cantucci over and bake for 10 minutes more. Remove the cantucci to a wire rack and let cool.

PAIRING The interplay of sweet Tuscan Vin Santo and the nutty crispness of these cookies is a traditional favorite; recommended producers include Fontodi, Capezzana, and Avignonesi.

About Fortified and Dessert Wines

While most fortified wines have a sweet character and go well with many types of desserts, not all fortified wines qualify as dessert wines. Conversely, a dessert wine is a naturally made wine that is not fortified and gets its sweetness from very ripe grapes that were left on the vines long into the growing season, and frequently beyond.

The term "fortified" indicates that brandy or some other neutral spirit was added to a wine during fermentation in order to accomplish two things: 1) to stop the alcoholic fermentation in its tracks, thus preserving any unconverted sugars (hence the sweetness mentioned above), and 2) to bring the alcohol level up to between 16 percent and 21 percent, thereby stabilizing the wine for years to come.

The best-known fortified wine is Port, which hails from the Douro Valley of Portugal. Port comes in several styles, led by vintage Port, which is made from grapes harvested in the same year. Fine vintage Ports should be structured and ageworthy. Tawny Ports are blended from several different vintages and aged for ten, twenty, or thirty or more years in large wood vats before bottling; unlike vintage Ports, tawny Ports are literally tawny in color and ready to drink upon release. Other styles of Port include late-bottled vintage and ruby, which are simpler, heavily-fruited wines made for early drinking.

Historic fortified wines that are similar to Port in style and stature include Madeira, which is made from white grapes and named for the Portuguese archipelago off the coast of Africa where it originates, and Marsala from the island of Sicily. Port-style wines have also become popular in Australia and California, two regions that have the warm growing climates necessary for making fortified wines.

Dessert wines, on the other hand, are not bolstered by the addition of brandy, and thus have much lower levels of alcohol but quite often an intense degree of sweetness. White grapes, more often than red ones, are used to make dessert wines, with Riesling, Pinot Blanc, Pinot Gris, Gewürztraminer, Moscatel, and Malvasia predominating. However, there are a small number of very good red-grape dessert wines made in countries that border the Mediterranean Sea, most notably Banyuls from France and Recioto della Valpolicella from Italy.

Typical food pairings for fortified wines include aged and blue cheeses, chocolate, and other sweets. Dessert wines, especially European wines made from Riesling, match up nicely with fruit-based desserts and custards.

Wine Classification Chart

CHAPTER 1:

Light, Aromatic White Wines

Albariño

Aligoté

Alvarinho

Arneis

Assyrtico

Chablis

Chasselas

Chenin Blanc

Colombard

Cortese

Ehrenfelser

Falanghina

Fiano

Folle Blanche

Fumé Blanc

Garganega

Gavi

Gewürztraminer

Godello

Greco di Tufo

Grillo

Grüner Veltliner

Hondarrabi Zuri

Insolia

Inzolia

Macon-Villages

Malagauzia

Malagousia

Malvasia

Melon

Moscato

Moschofilero

Müller-Thurgau

Muscadet

Pinot Blanc

Pinot Grigio

Pinot Gris

Pouilly-Fumé

Ribolla Gialla

Rieslaner

Riesling

Rkatsiteli

Roditis

Roter Veltliner

Sancerre

Sauvignon Blanc

Sauvignon Gris

Scheurebe

Sémillon

Seyval Blanc

Silvaner

Soave

Steen

Tocai Friulano

Torrontés

Traminer

Traminette

Trebbiano

Txakoli

Ugni Blanc

Verdejo

Verdicchio

Vermentino

Vernaccia

Viura

Weissburgunder

Welschriesling

Xarel-lo

CHAPTER 2:

Rich, Full-Bodied White Wines

Bordeaux (White)

Burgundy (White)

Chardonnay

Châteauneuf du Pape (White)

Condrieu

Côtes du Rhône (White)

Grenache Blanc

Marsanne

Roussanne

Viognier

CHAPTER 3:

Rosés and Light Red Wines

Beaujolais

Dolcetto

Freisa

Gamay

Lambrusco

Pinotage

Rosé

Valpolicella

CHAPTER 4:

Medium-Bodied, Fruit-Forward Red Wines

Agioritiko (St. George)

Baco Noir

Barbera

Bierzo

Bonarda

Burgundy (Red)

Cabernet Franc

Cannonau

Carmenère

Castelão

Charbono

Chianti

Cinsault

Côte-Rôtie

Côtes du Rhône (Red)

Crozes-Hermitage

Dornfelder

Garnacha

Grenache

Lagrein

Lemberger

Maréchal Foch

Mencía

Monastrell

Montepulciano

Negroamaro

Nero d'Avola

Norton

Pinot Noir

Sangiovese

Spätburgunder

St. George

St-Joseph

Teroldego

Touriga Franca

Trincadeira

Xinomavro

Zweigelt

CHAPTER 5:

Big, Powerful Red Wines

Aglianico

Amarone

Aragonés

Bandol

Barbaresco

Barolo

Bordeaux (Red)

Brunello di Montalcino

Cabernet Sauvignon

Carignan(e)

Carmignano

Chambourcin

Châteauneuf du Pape (Red)

Durif

Hermitage

Malbec

Mataro

Meritage

Merlot

Mondeuse

Mourvèdre

Nebbiolo

Petit Verdot

Petite Sirah

Primitivo

Ribera del Duero

Rioja

Sagrantino

Shiraz

Syrah

Tannat

Tempranillo

Tinta de Toro

Tinta Fina

Tinta Roriz

Tinto del Pais

Toro

Touriga Nacion

Zinfandel

CHAPTER 6:

Champagne & Sparkling Wines

Brachetto

Cava

Champagne

Prosecco

Sekt

CHAPTER 7:

Fortified and Dessert Wines

Banyuls

Beerenauslese

Eiswein (Icewine)

Madeira

Marsala

Muscat

Port

Sauternes

Sherry

Tawny Port

Tokay/Tokaji

Trockenbeerenauslese

Vin Santo

▶ Ch.	Wine/Grape/Region	Classification
4	Agioritiko (St. George)	Medium-Bodied, Fruit-Forward Red Wines
5	Aglianico	Big, Powerful Red Wines
1	Albariño	Light, Aromatic White Wines
1	Aligoté	Light, Aromatic White Wines
1	Alvarinho	Light, Aromatic White Wines
5	Amarone	Big, Powerful Red Wines
5	Aragonés	Big, Powerful Red Wines
1	Arneis	Light, Aromatic White Wines
1	Assyrtico	Light, Aromatic White Wines
4	Baco Noir	Medium-Bodied, Fruit-Forward Red Wines
5	Bandol	Big, Powerful Red Wines
7	Banyuls	Fortified and Dessert Wines
5	Barbaresco	Big, Powerful Red Wines
4	Barbera	Medium-Bodied, Fruit-Forward Red Wines
5	Barolo	Big, Powerful Red Wines
3	Beaujolais	Rosés and Light Red Wines
7	Beerenauslese	Fortified and Dessert Wines
4	Bierzo	Medium-Bodied, Fruit-Forward Red Wines
4	Bonarda	Medium-Bodied, Fruit-Forward Red Wines
5	Bordeaux (Red)	Big, Powerful Red Wines
2	Bordeaux (White)	Rich, Full-Bodied White Wines
6	Brachetto	Champagne and Sparkling Wines
5	Brunello di Montalcino	Big, Powerful Red Wines
4	Burgundy (Red)	Medium-Bodied, Fruit-Forward Red Wines
2	Burgundy (White)	Rich, Full-Bodied White Wines
4	Cabernet Franc	Medium-Bodied, Fruit-Forward Red Wines
5	Cabernet Sauvignon	Big, Powerful Red Wines
4	Cannonau	Medium-Bodied, Fruit-Forward Red Wines

5	Carignan(e)	Big, Powerful Red Wines
4	Carmenère	Medium-Bodied, Fruit-Forward Red Wines
5	Carmignano	Big, Powerful Red Wines
4	Castelão	Medium-Bodied, Fruit-Forward Red Wines
6	Cava	Champagne and Sparkling Wines
1	Chablis	Light, Aromatic White Wines
5	Chambourcin	Big, Powerful Red Wines
6	Champagne	Champagne and Sparkling Wines
4	Charbono	Medium-Bodied, Fruit-Forward Red Wines
2	Chardonnay	Rich, Full-Bodied White Wines
1	Chasselas	Light, Aromatic White Wines
5	Châteauneuf du Pape (Red)	Big, Powerful Red Wines
2	Châteauneuf du Pape (White)	Rich, Full-Bodied White Wines
1	Chenin Blanc	Light, Aromatic White Wines
4	Chianti	Medium-Bodied, Fruit-Forward Red Wines
4	Cinsault	Medium-Bodied, Fruit-Forward Red Wines
1	Colombard	Light, Aromatic White Wines
2	Condrieu	Rich, Full-Bodied White Wines
1	Cortese	Light, Aromatic White Wines
4	Côte-Rôtie	Medium-Bodied, Fruit-Forward Red Wines
4	Côtes du Rhône (Red)	Medium-Bodied, Fruit-Forward Red Wines
2	Côtes du Rhône (White)	Rich, Full-Bodied White Wines
4	Crozes-Hermitage	Medium-Bodied, Fruit-Forward Red Wines
3	Dolcetto	Rosés and Light Red Wines
4	Dornfelder	Medium-Bodied, Fruit-Forward Red Wines
5	Durif	Big, Powerful Red Wines
1	Ehrenfelser	Light, Aromatic White Wines
7	Eiswein (Icewine)	Fortified and Dessert Wines
1	Falanghina	Light, Aromatic White Wines
1	Fiano	Light, Aromatic White Wines

1	Folle Blanche	Light, Aromatic White Wines
3	Freisa	Rosés and Light Red Wines
1	Fumé Blanc	Light, Aromatic White Wines
3	Gamay	Rosés and Light Red Wines
1	Garganega	Light, Aromatic White Wines
4	Garnacha	Medium-Bodied, Fruit-Forward Red Wines
1	Gavi	Light, Aromatic White Wines
1	Gewürztraminer	Light, Aromatic White Wines
1	Godello	Light, Aromatic White Wines
1	Greco di Tufo	Light, Aromatic White Wines
4	Grenache	Medium-Bodied, Fruit-Forward Red Wines
2	Grenache Blanc	Rich, Full-Bodied White Wines
1	Grillo	Light, Aromatic White Wines
1	Grüner Veltliner	Light, Aromatic White Wines
5	Hermitage	Big, Powerful Red Wines
1	Hondarrabi Zuri	Light, Aromatic White Wines
1	Insolia	Light, Aromatic White Wines
1	Inzolia	Light, Aromatic White Wines
4	Lagrein	Medium-Bodied, Fruit-Forward Red Wines
3	Lambrusco	Rosés and Light Red Wines
4	Lemberger	Medium-Bodied, Fruit-Forward Red Wines
1	Macon-Villages	Light, Aromatic White Wines
7	Madeira	Fortified and Dessert Wines
1	Malagauzia	Light, Aromatic White Wines
1	Malagousia	Light, Aromatic White Wines
5	Malbec	Big, Powerful Red Wines
1	Malvasia	Light, Aromatic White Wines
4	Maréchal Foch	Medium-Bodied, Fruit-Forward Red Wines
7	Marsala	Fortified and Dessert Wines
2	Marsanne	Rich, Full-Bodied White Wines
5	Mataro	Big, Powerful Red Wines

1	Melon	Light, Aromatic White Wines
4	Mencía	Medium-Bodied, Fruit-Forward Red Wines
5	Meritage	Big, Powerful Red Wines
5	Merlot	Big, Powerful Red Wines
4	Monastrell	Medium-Bodied, Fruit-Forward Red Wines
5	Mondeuse	Big, Powerful Red Wines
4	Montepulciano	Medium-Bodied, Fruit-Forward Red Wines
1	Moscato	Light, Aromatic White Wines
1	Moschofilero	Light, Aromatic White Wines
5	Mourvèdre	Big, Powerful Red Wines
1	Müller-Thurgau	Light, Aromatic White Wines
1	Muscadet	Light, Aromatic White Wines
7	Muscat	Fortified and Dessert Wines
5	Nebbiolo	Big, Powerful Red Wines
4	Negroamaro	Medium-Bodied, Fruit-Forward Red Wines
4	Nero d'Avola	Medium-Bodied, Fruit-Forward Red Wines
4	Norton	Medium-Bodied, Fruit-Forward Red Wines
5	Petit Verdot	Big, Powerful Red Wines
5	Petite Sirah	Big, Powerful Red Wines
1	Pinot Blanc	Light, Aromatic White Wines
1	Pinot Grigio	Light, Aromatic White Wines
1	Pinot Gris	Light, Aromatic White Wines
4	Pinot Noir	Medium-Bodied, Fruit-Forward Red Wines
3	Pinotage	Rosés and Light Red Wines
7	Port	Fortified and Dessert Wines
1	Pouilly-Fumé	Light, Aromatic White Wines
5	Primitivo	Big, Powerful Red Wines
6	Prosecco	Champagne and Sparkling Wines
5	Ribera del Duero	Big, Powerful Red Wines
1	Ribolla Gialla	Light, Aromatic White Wines
1	Rieslaner	Light, Aromatic White Wines

1	Riesling	Light, Aromatic White Wines
5	Rioja	Big, Powerful Red Wines
1	Rkatsiteli	Light, Aromatic White Wines
1	Roditis	Light, Aromatic White Wines
3	Rosé	Rosés and Light Red Wines
1	Roter Veltliner	Light, Aromatic White Wines
2	Roussanne	Rich, Full-Bodied White Wines
5	Sagrantino	Big, Powerful Red Wines
1	Sancerre	Light, Aromatic White Wines
4	Sangiovese	Medium-Bodied, Fruit-Forward Red Wines
7	Sauternes	Fortified and Dessert Wines
1	Sauvignon Blanc	Light, Aromatic White Wines
1	Sauvignon Gris	Light, Aromatic White Wines
1	Scheurebe	Light, Aromatic White Wines
6	Sekt	Champagne and Sparkling Wines
1	Sémillon	Light, Aromatic White Wines
1	Seyval Blanc	Light, Aromatic White Wines
7	Sherry	Fortified and Dessert Wines
5	Shiraz	Big, Powerful Red Wines
1	Silvaner	Light, Aromatic White Wines
1	Soave	Light, Aromatic White Wines
4	Spätburgunder	Medium-Bodied, Fruit-Forward Red Wines
4	St. George	Medium-Bodied, Fruit-Forward Red Wines
1	Steen	Light, Aromatic White Wines
4	St-Joseph	Medium-Bodied, Fruit-Forward Red Wines
5	Syrah	Big, Powerful Red Wines
5	Tannat	Big, Powerful Red Wines
7	Tawny Port	Fortified and Dessert Wines
5	Tempranillo	Big, Powerful Red Wines
4	Teroldego	Medium-Bodied, Fruit-Forward Red Wines
5	Tinta de Toro	Big, Powerful Red Wines

5	Tinta Fina	Big, Powerful Red Wines
5	Tinta Roriz	Big, Powerful Red Wines
5	Tinto del Pais	Big, Powerful Red Wines
1	Tocai Friulano	Light, Aromatic White Wines
7	Tokay/Tokaji	Fortified and Dessert Wines
5	Toro	Big, Powerful Red Wines
1	Torrontés	Light, Aromatic White Wines
4	Touriga Franca	Medium-Bodied, Fruit-Forward Red Wines
5	Touriga Nacion	Big, Powerful Red Wines
1	Traminer	Light, Aromatic White Wines
1	Traminette	Light, Aromatic White Wines
1	Trebbiano	Light, Aromatic White Wines
4	Trincadeira	Medium-Bodied, Fruit-Forward Red Wines
7	Trockenbeerenauslese	Fortified and Dessert Wines
1	Txakoli	Light, Aromatic White Wines
1	Ugni Blanc	Light, Aromatic White Wines
3	Valpolicella	Rosés and Light Red Wines
1	Verdejo	Light, Aromatic White Wines
1	Verdicchio	Light, Aromatic White Wines
1	Vermentino	Light, Aromatic White Wines
1	Vernaccia	Light, Aromatic White Wines
7	Vin Santo	Fortified and Dessert Wines
2	Viognier	Rich, Full-Bodied White Wines
1	Viura	Light, Aromatic White Wines
1	Weissburgunder	Light, Aromatic White Wines
1	Welschriesling	Light, Aromatic White Wines
1	Xarel-lo	Light, Aromatic White Wines
4	Xinomavro	Medium-Bodied, Fruit-Forward Red Wines
5	Zinfandel	Big, Powerful Red Wines
4	Zweigelt	Medium-Bodied, Fruit-Forward Red Wines

Credits

CHAPTER 1

Light, Aromatic White Wines

"Mussels Provençal" published in "A Mediterranean Brunch" by Karen Berman, *Wine Enthusiast Magazine*, March 2004. Reprinted with permission.

"Totally Nuts Chicken Saté Burgers" from *Burgers Every Way* by Emily Haft Bloom (Stewart, Tabori and Chang, 2004), published in "Burgers Without Borders" by Emily Haft Bloom, *Wine Enthusiast Magazine*, September 2007. Reprinted with permission.

"Spaghetti with Cockles and Parsley" adapted from recipe in *The Flavors of Southern Italy* by Erica De Mane (Wiley, 2004), published in "Powerhouse Pastas" by Toni Lydecker, *Wine Enthusiast Magazine*, December 15, 2005. Reprinted with permission.

"Wild Mushroom Hunter's Soup" adapted from recipe in *Cooking One-on-One* by John Ash (Clarkson Potter, 2004), published in "Exotic Mushrooms" by Steve Heimoff, *Wine Enthusiast Magazine*, November 1, 2005. Reprinted with permission.

"Chilled Cucumber Water with Minted Crab Salad" courtesy of Chef Michael Allemeier, Mission Hill Family Estate (Okanagan Valley, British Columbia), published in "Soup for Summer" by Karen Berman, *Wine Enthusiast Magazine*, August 2006. Reprinted with permission.

"Vietnamese-Style Steak Salad" published in "Vino al Fresco" by Toni Lydecker, *Wine Enthusiast Magazine*, June 2006. Reprinted with permission.

"Chicken and Citrus Slaw Tostadas" from *Cowgirl Cuisine* by Paula Disbrowe (HarperCollins, 2007), published in "The Enth Degree Recipe of the Month," *Wine Enthusiast Magazine*, August 2007. Reprinted with permission.

"Paella de Pollo y Setas" from *Tapas: A Taste of Spain* in America, by Jose Andrés with Richard Wolfe (Clarkson Potter, 2006), published in "Setting Your Own Spanish Table" by Michael Schachner, *Wine Enthusiast Magazine*, October 2007. Reprinted with permission.

"Linguini all' Istriana" published in "Pasta e Vino" by Lidia Bastianich, *Wine Enthusiast Magazine*, April 2003. Reprinted with permission.

"Pork Loin with Cider-Madeira Sauce" adapted from recipe at www.cooks.com, published in "Cooking with Fortified Wines" by Michael Schachner, *Wine Enthusiast Magazine*, November 15, 2006. Reprinted with permission.

"Avocado, Tomato, and Spinach Crêpes with Bacon and Pesto" published in "Avocados Beyond Guacamole" by Gretchen Roberts, *Wine Enthusiast Magazine*, July 2007. Reprinted with permission.

"Crispy Fried Artichokes" adapted from recipe by Chef Anna Dente Ferracci, Osteria di San Cesario (Rome, Italy), published in "Never Say Never" by Monica Larner, *Wine Enthusiast Magazine*, June 2007. Reprinted with permission.

"Pesto alla Genovese," courtesy of Chef Antonio Amato, Osteria Creuza de Mä (Genoa, Italy), published in "Pesto Three Ways" by Monica Larner, *Wine Enthusiast Magazine*, May 2006. Reprinted with permission.

CHAPTER 2

Rich, Full-Bodied White Wines

"Chilled Corn Soup with Crab and Scallions," "Tomato Gazpacho with Avocado and Lobster," and "Sweet Pea Soup with Warm Lardons," courtesy of Chef Jeff Raider, Valley Restaurant at the Garrison (Garrison, NY), published in "The Enth Degree Recipe of the Month: Trio of Summer Soups," *Wine Enthusiast Magazine*, July 2006. Reprinted with permission.

"Maine Lobster Salad," courtesy of Executive Chef David Daniels, formerly of The Federalist, XV Beacon Hotel (Boston, MA), currently of Topper's Restaurant at The Wauwinet (Nantucket, MA), published in "Behind the Scenes Under the Sea" by Melanie Barnard, *Wine Enthusiast Magazine*, July 2005. Reprinted with permission.

"Garlic and Portobello Soup with Goat Cheese and White Truffle Oil," courtesy of Chef Cal Stamenov, Marinus Restaurant at Bernardus Lodge (Carmel Valley, CA), published in "Winery Chefs' Spring Time Dinner" by Steve Heimoff, *Wine Enthusiast Magazine*, May 2007. Reprinted with permission.

"Summer Squash Soup with Basil and Parmesan," adapted from recipe in *Keep It Seasonal: Soups, Salads and Sandwiches* by Annie Wayte (William Morrow, 2006), published in "Soup for Summer" by Karen Berman, *Wine Enthusiast Magazine*, August 2006. Reprinted with permission.

"Pastel de Jaibas" is a combination of two separate recipes by Chef Pilar Rodriguez, Comida y Vino (Pichilemu, Chile) and Chef Jorge Pacheco, Aquí Está Coco (Santiago, Chile), published in "Chile's Hearty Cuisine" by Michael Schachner, *Wine Enthusiast Magazine*, October 2006. Reprinted with permission.

"Grilled Whole Red Snapper with Grilled Fennel and Ratatouille," adapted from recipe by Chef Rick Moonen, formerly of Oceana (New York, NY), currently chef/owner of RM Seafood (Las Vegas, NV) published in "Beyond White Wine with Fish" by Karen Berman, *Wine Enthusiast Magazine*, July 2002. Reprinted with permission.

"Wrapped Oyster Fritters with Apple-Mint Chutney and Passion Fruit Sauce," courtesy of Chef Barak Hirschowitz (www.sachef.com, Cape Town, South Africa), published in "Bite-Size Meals" by Roger Voss, *Wine Enthusiast Magazine*, November 15, 2005. Reprinted with permission.

"Lobster à l'Americaine with Basmati-Risotto Cakes," courtesy of Chef Didier Virot, Aix (New York, NY), published in "Rice Mixes It Up" by Melissa Clark, *Wine Enthusiast Magazine*, December 15, 2003. Reprinted with permission.

"Dungeness Crab Salad with Roasted Beets, Arugula, and Blood Orange Vinaigrette," courtesy of Chef Jerry Regester, The Restaurant at Wente Vineyards (Livermore, CA), published in "Winery Chefs' Spring Time Dinner" by Steve Heimoff, *Wine Enthusiast Magazine*, May 2007. Reprinted with permission.

"Confit of Tuna with Onion Confit, Endive Salad, and Sauce Verte," adapted from recipe in *The Farallon Cookbook* by Mark Franz and Lisa Weiss (Chronicle, 2001), published in "Beyond White Wine" with Fish by Karen Berman, *Wine Enthusiast Magazine*, July 2002. Reprinted with permission.

CHAPTER 3

Rosés and Light Red Wines

"Summer Tomato Salad" published in "Salad Days" by Michele Anna Jordan, *Wine Enthusiast Magazine*, August 2003. Reprinted with permission.

"Pan Bagnat" published in "Vino al Fresco" by Toni Lydecker, *Wine Enthusiast Magazine*, June 2006. Reprinted with permission.

"Provençal Soupe au Pistou" courtesy of Restaurant Galerie des Arcades (Biot, France), published in "Pesto Three Ways" by Monica Larner, *Wine Enthusiast Magazine*, May 2006. Reprinted with permission.

"Vintner Grill's Bouillabaisse" courtesy of Executive Chef Matthew Silverman, Vintner Grill (Las Vegas, NV), published in "The Enth Degree: Recipe of the Month," *Wine Enthusiast Magazine*, July 2007. Reprinted with permission from chef.

"Tuna 'alla Napoletana' with Osetra Caviar," courtesy of Chef Chris Manning, Étoile at Domaine Chandon (Yountsville, CA), published in "Winery Chefs' Spring Time Dinner" by Steve Heimoff, *Wine Enthusiast Magazine*, May 2007. Reprinted with permission.

"Moroccan-style Lamb Shanks with Olives and Preserved Lemons" published in Sheer Lamb by Michele Anna Jordan, *Wine Enthusiast Magazine*, December 1, 2005. Reprinted with permission.

CHAPTER 4

Medium-Bodied, Fruit-Forward Red Wines

"Perfect Portobello and Red Pepper 'Almost' Burgers" from *Burgers Every Way* by Emily Haft Bloom (Stewart, Tabori and Chang, 2004), published in "Burgers Without Borders" by Emily Haft Bloom, *Wine Enthusiast Magazine*, September 2007. Reprinted with permission.

"Pork Chops with Pinot Noir and Espresso Demi-Glace" published in "Coffee Chic" by Margaret Shakespeare, *Wine Enthusiast Magazine*, November 15, 2000. Reprinted with permission.

"Wild Rice Salad with Mushrooms, Cranberries, and Walnut Oil," courtesy of Chef Alfred Portale, Gotham Bar and Grill (New York, NY), published in "Rice Mixes It Up" by Melissa Clark, *Wine Enthusiast Magazine*, December 15, 2003. Reprinted with permission.

"Lamb and Cherry Kebabs from Aleppo," adapted from a recipe in *Little Foods of the Mediterranean* by Clifford A. Wright (The Harvard Common Press, 2003), published in "Middle East Meets West" by Karen Berman, *Wine Enthusiast Magazine*, November 15, 2007. Reprinted with permission.

"Grilled Salmon with Olive Butter and Orzo" published in "The Extraordinary Olive" by Michele Anna Jordan, *Wine Enthusiast Magazine*, August 2002. Reprinted with permission.

"Roasted Golden Beets with Olives" published in "The Extraordinary Olive" by Michele Anna Jordan, *Wine Enthusiast Magazine*, August 2002. Reprinted with permission.

"Duck Breast with Caramelized Apples and Lavender Honey" courtesy of Tartine Restaurant (Westport, CT), published in "The Bistro Is Back" by Mary Hunt, *Wine Enthusiast Magazine*, December 31, 2000. Reprinted with permission.

"Uighur Autumn Pulao" from *Seductions of Rice* by Jeffrey Alford and Naomi Duguid (Artisan, 1998), published in "Rice Mixes It Up" by Melissa Clark, *Wine Enthusiast Magazine*, December 15, 2003. Reprinted with permission.

"Sali Boti," adapted from recipe by Chef Ashok Bajaj, Bombay Club (Washington, D.C.), published in "Passage to India" by Karen Berman, *Wine Enthusiast Magazine*, March 2005. Reprinted with permission.

"Caldo de Camarón Asado" adapted from recipe in *Mexico: One Plate at a Time* by Rick Bayless (Scribner, 2000), published in "Traductor" by Daryna McKeand Tobey, *Wine Enthusiast Magazine*, December 15, 2002. Reprinted with permission.

"Pozole de Pato," adapted from recipe in *Modern Mexican Flavors* by Richard Sandoval (Harry N. Abrams Inc, 2002), published in "Soup for Summer" by Karen Berman, *Wine Enthusiast Magazine*, August 2006. Reprinted with permission.

"Aglaia's Moussaka," from *New Greek Cuisine* by Jim Botsacos (Broadway Books, 2006), published in "Greece Bears Gifts" by Karen Berman, *Wine Enthusiast Magazine*, December 2007. Reprinted with permission.

"Roasted Asparagus with Aceto Balsamico Tradizionale di Modena" published in "Never Say Never" by Monica Larner, *Wine Enthusiast Magazine*, June 2007. Reprinted with permission.

CHAPTER 5
Big, Powerful Red Wines

"Churrasco for Those Who Don't Live in Mansions" published in "Brazil on the Front Burner" by Tara Gadomski, *Wine Enthusiast Magazine*, March 2007. Reprinted with permission.

"Slow Cooked Rack of Lamb" published in "Sheer Lamb" by Michele Anna Jordan, *Wine Enthusiast Magazine*, December 1, 2005. Reprinted with permission.

"Steak Frites" courtesy of Josh Moulton, formerly of Bleu (Greenwich, CT), published in "The Bistro Is Back" by Mary Hunt, *Wine Enthusiast Magazine*, December 31, 2000. Reprinted with permission.

"Vella's Pasta alla Campagna" courtesy of Ig Vella, Vella Cheese Company (Sonoma, CA), from *The New Cook's Tour of Sonoma* by Michele Anna Jordan (Sasquatch Books, 2000), excerpted in "The New Cook's Tour of Sonoma" by Michele Anna Jordan, *Wine Enthusiast Magazine*, July 2000. Reprinted with permission.

"Lamb Shanks in Red Wine with Pomegranate and Mint Gremolata" adapted from a recipe in *The Plumpjack Cookbook: Recipes for Living Well* by Jeff Morgan (Rodale Press, 2006), published in "A Night Different From All Other Nights" by Jeff Morgan, *Wine Enthusiast Magazine*, April 2006. Reprinted with permission.

"Roast Duckling with Merlot-Chocolate Sauce and Roasted Beets" courtesy of David Page, Home Restaurant (New York, NY), published in "Delicious Duck Recipes" (online companion to Bird on a Wire) by Karen Berman, *Wine Enthusiast Magazine*, November 1, 2006. Reprinted with permission.

"Tournedos au Bleu with Potatoes au Gratin and Sautéed Green Beans" courtesy of Chef Eric Masson, formerly of Saratoga Lake Inn (Saratoga, NY), currently of The Brentwood (Little River, SC), published in "Rules for Blues" by Karen Berman, *Wine Enthusiast Magazine*, December 31, 2005. Reprinted with permission.

"Baked Rigatoni with Eggplant and Sausage" published in "Powerhouse Pastas" by Toni Lydecker, *Wine Enthusiast Magazine*, December 15, 2005. Reprinted with permission.

"Cassoulet des Pyrénées" published in "A Taste of Gascony" by F. Paul Pacult, *Wine Enthusiast Magazine*, December 31, 2006. Reprinted with permission.

"Orecchiette with Dandelion Greens and Chickpeas" published in "Powerhouse Pastas" by Toni Lydecker, *Wine Enthusiast Magazine*, December 15, 2005. Reprinted with permission.

CHAPTER 6.
Champagne and Sparkling Wines

"Marinated Baby Lamb Chops with Mango Chutney," courtesy of Chef Daniel Escarament, formerly of the yacht Cookie Monster, published in "Hors D'Oeuvres That Sparkle" by Mary Hunt, *Wine Enthusiast Magazine*, December 1, 2000. Reprinted with permission.

"Smoked Salmon and Caviar Croque Monsieur," adapted from a recipe by Chef Eric Ripert, Le Bernardin (New York, NY), published in "The Ultimate New Year's Eve" by Florence Fabricant, *Wine Enthusiast Magazine*, December 15, 2000. Reprinted with permission.

"Raspberry Phyllo Cups with Brie," courtesy of Elizabeth Parri Butler, Perfect Parties, Inc. and Elizabeth's Café (Madison, CT), published in "Tasty Tidbits for Holiday Entertaining" by Karen Berman, *Wine Enthusiast Magazine*, December 15, 2001. Reprinted with permission.

"Chicken Liver Pâté," courtesy of Executive Chef Laurent Tourondel, BLT Group (New York, NY), published in "Cooking with Fortified Wines" by Michael Schachner, *Wine Enthusiast Magazine*, November 2006. Reprinted with permission.

"Summer Melon Salad with Prosciutto" published in "Salad Days" by Michele Anna Jordan, *Wine Enthusiast Magazine*, August 2003. Reprinted with permission.

"Duck Breast with Spaetzle, Chanterelles, and Spinach Purée," courtesy of Executive Chef Brian Bistrong, formerly of Citarella (New York, NY), published in "Sparkling Nights" by Melissa Clark, *Wine Enthusiast Magazine*, December 1, 2003. Reprinted with permission.

"Grilled Mushroom and Citrus Salad with Bucheret," adapted from recipe in *Cooking One-on-One* by John Ash (Clarkson Potter, 2004), published in "Exotic Mushrooms" by Steve Heimoff, *Wine Enthusiast Magazine*, November 1, 2005. Reprinted with permission.

"Velveteen Corn Soup with Cornbread Croutons, Caviar, and Crème Fraîche" published in "Sublime Soups" by Karen Berman, *Wine Enthusiast Magazine*, December 15, 2004. Reprinted with permission.

"Hearty Frittata with Potatoes, Red Pepper, Porcini Mushrooms, and Turkey Chorizo" published in "A Mediterranean Brunch" by Karen Berman, *Wine Enthusiast Magazine*, March 2004. Reprinted with permission.

"Frozen Champagne Elderflower Soup with White Peaches," courtesy of Pastry Chef William Yosses, Citarella (New York, NY), published in "Sparkling Nights" by Melissa Clark, *Wine Enthusiast Magazine*, December 1, 2003. Reprinted with permission.

"Mediterranean Green Salad with Herbs and Fennel" published in "Salad Days" by Michele Anna Jordan, *Wine Enthusiast Magazine*, August 2003. Reprinted with permission.

CHAPTER 7

Fortified and Dessert Wines

"Chorizo and Shrimp with Palo Cortado" adapted from "Chorizo Sausages with Shrimps" at www.tenstartapas.com, by Chef Angela Hartnett, formerly of The Connaught (London, UK), currently of Cielo (Boca Raton, FL), published in "Cooking with Fortified Wines" by Michael Schachner, *Wine Enthusiast Magazine*, November 15, 2006. Reprinted with permission.

"BBQ Duck–Filled Blue Corn Pancakes with Habañero Sauce" first published in *Bobby Flay's Mesa Grill Cookbook: Explosive Flavors from the Southwestern Kitchen* by Bobby Flay with Stephanie Banyas and Sally Jackson. Copyright © 2007 by Boy Meets Grill, Inc. All rights reserved. Published in the United States by Clarkson Potter/Publishers, an imprint of the Crown Publishing Group, a division of Random House, Inc, New York.

"Frontera's Chocolate Pecan Pie Bars" adapted from recipe in *Salsas That Cook* by Rick Bayless (Scribner, 1998), published in "Traductor" by Daryna McKeand, *Wine Enthusiast Magazine*, December 15, 2002. Reprinted with permission.

"Warm Chocolate Soufflé" adapted from recipe in *Simply Sensational Desserts* by François Payard (Broadway Books, 1999), published in "Love Is in the Air" by Karen Berman, *Wine Enthusiast Magazine* Online, February 2007. Reprinted with permission.

"Warm Chocolate Cakes with Dulce De Leche" first published in *Bobby Flay's Mesa Grill Cookbook: Explosive Flavors from the Southwestern Kitchen* by Bobby Flay with Stephanie Banyas and Sally Jackson. Copyright © 2007 by Boy Meets Grill, Inc. All rights reserved. Published in the United States by Clarkson Potter/Publishers, an imprint of the Crown Publishing Group, a division of Random House, Inc, New York.

"Spiced-Rum Cake with Caramel-Rum Frosting and Candied Walnuts" published in "Frosting on the Cake" by Mary Goodbody, *Wine Enthusiast Magazine*, February 2006. Reprinted with permission.

"Wild Mushroom and Tomato Risotto," published in "Sherry Course by Course" by Michael Schachner, *Wine Enthusiast Magazine*, October 2003. Reprinted with permission.

"Asparagus in Foie Gras Phyllo Packages," courtesy of Chef Georges Gotrand (Bordeaux, France), published in "Bite-Size Meals" by Roger Voss, *Wine Enthusiast Magazine*, November

"Pears Poached in Armagnac with Vanilla Ice Cream" published in "A Taste of Gascony" by F. Paul Pacult, *Wine Enthusiast Magazine*, December 31, 2006. Reprinted with permission.

"Roquefort Shortbread," courtesy of Chef Georges Gotrand (Bordeaux, France), published in "Bite-Size Meals" by Roger Voss, *Wine Enthusiast Magazine*, November 15, 2005. Reprinted with permission.

"Crema Catalana with Bay Leaf Buñuelos," courtesy of Chef Andy Nusser, Casa Mono (New York, NY), published in "Setting Your Own Spanish Table" by Michael Schachner, *Wine Enthusiast Magazine*, October 2007. Reprinted with permission.

"White Chocolate Rice Pudding," courtesy of Pastry Chef Mimi Young, formerly of Scala's Bistro (San Francisco, CA), currently of Palio (San Francisco, CA), published in "Rice Mixes It Up" by Melissa Clark, *Wine Enthusiast Magazine*, December 15, 2003. Reprinted with permission.

"Tuscany's Cantucci," courtesy of Biscottificio Antonio Mattei (Prato, Italy), published in "La Dolce Vita" by Monica Larner, *Wine Enthusiast Magazine*, June 2005. Reprinted with permission.

Conversion Tables

FORMULAS FOR METRIC CONVERSION

Ounces to grams
multiply ounces by 28.35

Pounds to grams
multiply pounds by 453.5

Cups to liters
multiply cups by .24

Fahrenheit to Centigrade
subtract 32 from Fahrenheit,
multiply by five and divide by 9

METRIC EQUIVALENTS FOR VOLUME

U.S.		Metric
⅛ tsp.		0.6 ml
½ tsp.		2.5 ml
¾ tsp.		4.0 ml
1 tsp.		5.0 ml
1 ½ tsp.		7.0 ml
2 tsp.		10.0 ml
3 tsp.		15.0 ml
4 tsp.		20.0 ml
1 Tbsp.	—	15.0 ml
1 ½ Tbsp.	—	22.0 ml
2 Tbsp. (⅛ cup)	1 fl. oz	30.0 ml
2 ½ Tbsp.	—	37.0 ml
3 Tbsp.	—	44.0 ml
⅓ cup	—	57.0 ml
4 Tbsp. (¼ cup)	2 fl. oz	59.0 ml
5 Tbsp.	—	74.0 ml
6 Tbsp.	—	89.0 ml
8 Tbsp. (½ cup)	4 fl. oz	120.0 ml
¾ cup	6 fl. oz	178.0 ml
1 cup	8 fl. oz	237.0 ml (.24 liters)
1 ½ cups	—	354.0 ml
1 ¾ cups	—	414.0 ml
2 cups (1 pint)	16 fl. oz	473.0 ml
4 cups (1 quart)	32 fl. oz	(.95 liters)
5 cups	—	(1.183 liters)
16 cups (1 gallon)	128 fl. oz	(3.8 liters)

OVEN TEMPERATURES

Degrees Fahrenheit	Degrees Centigrade	British Gas Marks
200°	93°	—
250°	120°	—
275°	140°	1
300°	150°	2
325°	165°	3
350°	175°	4
375°	190°	5
400°	200°	6
450°	230°	8

METRIC EQUIVALENTS FOR BUTTER

U.S.	Metric
2 tsp.	10.0 g
1 Tbsp.	15.0 g
1 ½ Tbsp.	22.5 g
2 Tbsp. (1 oz)	55.0 g
3 Tbsp.	70.0 g
¼ lb. (1 stick)	110.0 g
½ lb. (2 sticks)	220.0 g

METRIC EQUIVALENTS FOR WEIGHT

U.S.	Metric
1 oz	28 g
2 oz	58 g
3 oz	85 g
4 oz (¼ lb.)	113 g
5 oz	142 g
6 oz	170 g
7 oz	199 g
8 oz (½ lb.)	227 g
10 oz	284 g
12 oz (¾ lb.)	340 g
14 oz	397 g
16 oz (1 lb.)	454 g

METRIC EQUIVALENTS FOR LENGTH

U.S.	Metric
¼ inch	.65 cm
½ inch	1.25 cm
1 inch	2.50 cm
2 inches	5.00 cm
3 inches	6.00 cm
4 inches	8.00 cm
5 inches	11.00 cm
6 inches	15.00 cm
7 inches	18.00 cm
8 inches	20.00 cm
9 inches	23.00 cm
12 inches	30.50 cm
15 inches	38.00 cm

INDEX